INTRODUCTION TO TRANSPORTATION PLANNING

M. J. BRUTON
B.A., M.SC., D.I.C., Dip.T.P., A.M.T.P.I., A.M.I.H.E.
*Principal Lecturer in Town Planning,
School of Town Planning, Oxford College of Technology*

HUTCHINSON TECHNICAL EDUCATION

HUTCHINSON EDUCATIONAL LTD
178–202 Great Portland Street, London W1

London Melbourne Sydney
Auckland Bombay Toronto
Johannesburg New York

First published 1970

*This book has been set in Garamond, printed in Great Britain
on Smooth Wove paper by Anchor Press, and
bound by Wm. Brendon, both of Tiptree, Essex*

09 098620 2

For Sheila and 'Lou'

Acknowledgements

The author would like to thank all those who gave permission for use of copyright material in the text, in particular to the City of Cardiff Corporation and to Colin Buchanan and Partners in association with W. S. Atkins for their consent to the use in Chapter 3 of trip generation equations derived in connection with the Cardiff Study. He would also like to thank Cesar Marquez who drew all the diagrams for the book.

Contents

Preface

The land use – transportation planning process can be sub-divided in very general terms into four main stages:

1. The estimation of future demands for movement, and the establishment of the shortcomings in the existing transportation system to meet this future demand.

2. The design of a series of alternative transportation plans which accord with community aims and objectives and meet this estimated demand for movement.

3. The evaluation of alternative transportation plans, in both economic and social terms, to derive the optimum solution.

4. The financing and implementation of the chosen alternative plan.

The procedure is complex and highly involved, dealing with and attempting to quantify for some future date the wishes and demands of people.

This book deals only with the techniques of estimating future demands for movement. As such it can be considered to provide an introduction to both traffic estimation procedures, and the transportation planning process. Although methods of evaluating alternative proposals are touched on, the major aim of the book is to outline, in as simple a way as possible, the traffic estimation procedure, highlighting the problems and shortcomings associated with it.

No attempt is made to cover, what in my opinion constitute

the more important and intractable problems associated with route location, the setting up of community goals and objectives, and the implementation of the chosen alternative. The present state of the art is such that the true significance of these aspects is only gradually being recognized. However, the furore aroused by transportation proposals recently put forward in some of the towns and cities of this country, indicates that much more attention must be given to the problems associated with goal setting, public participation and route location, before the transportation planning process as a whole can be considered to be successful.

1 Introduction

'Efficient transportation has become one of the major challenges confronting the modern urban region, since the vitality of an urban region relates directly to the quality of its transportation services. Few other issues are so long-term in their impact or so controversial in their solution' (*Transportation and Parking for Tomorrow's Cities*, Wilbur Smith and Associates, New Haven, Connecticut, 1966)

Need for movement studies

The problem of providing an adequate transportation system in the urban areas of the world is not a new one. In an attempt to relieve congestion in Rome, in the first century A.D. vehicular traffic (with the exception of chariots and state vehicles) was restricted to the hours of darkness. Congestion was commonplace in seventeenth-century London, and nineteenth-century New York. It has always existed wherever large numbers of people have congregated in limited areas, but it was not until the process of urbanisation and industrialisation was well under way, in the nineteenth century, that problems of vehicular traffic in towns began to take on a serious dimension. This process of urbanisation has been rapid—prior to 1850 no society could be described as predominantly urban; by 1900 only Great Britain could be so regarded. Today, in 1969, all the world's industrial nations are highly urbanised—approximately 80% of the population of England and Wales is defined as urban, 70% of the population of the U.S.A. is defined as urban, and 65% of the population of Japan.

In parallel with this process of urbanisation and the growth of towns and cities has been the development of transportation —from foot and horse to railway, tram, bus and private motor vehicle. The successive introduction of these new transport forms over the past century has done much to influence and assist in the change from an agrarian to an urban society. But the introduction of these new transport forms has occurred in a far more rapid sequence than the traditional cycles of urban renewal. With the result that the majority of towns and cities in the world today are not designed or equipped to cope with, or realise the potential of, the new transport media. The *Traffic in Towns Report* established this point quite emphatically.

'The manner in which the buildings and streets are put together is basically unsuitable for motor traffic. This soon became apparent after the invention of the motor vehicle because it soon exerted a strong influence towards changing the form of towns by encouraging the outward spread and sprawl of development.'[1]

As if this were not enough, the problem has been further complicated by rapidly improving living standards. The desire for more congenial and comfortable living conditions, and the ability to pay for these improvements, has affected the individual's choice of residence and mode of travel. It could be argued that 'the transportation plight of cities—at least in the prosperous and developed countries of the world—is a condition people have themselves brought about by taking advantage of individual opportunities'.[2] Although this rate of growth and change within the world's urban areas has been rapid in the past century, it must be recognised that future decades will see equally dramatic new developments. An urban transportation system capable of moving goods and people from place to place in a socially acceptable and economically feasible manner, is an essential part of this shifting scene. Again it was the *Traffic in Towns Report* which firmly established in this country that

> 'in all consideration of urban form . . . the question of facility of movement of both persons and goods is of crucial importance. It deserves far more attention than has been bestowed upon it in the past; indeed it can be said that it must now become one of the prime factors in the determination of where population and activities are to be settled. If this is to be the case, however, a much greater understanding of the relationship between various kinds of development and the demands for movement which they generate, needs to be developed. . . . It is important that movement demands be studied as a whole . . . because all the indications . . . are that in a complex community no single system of transport can provide for all the movements involved, and that coordination between systems is required.'[3]

Early development of Movement Studies

1 *North America*

Prior to the early fifties problems of movement were seen largely in terms of road traffic, and the accepted method of assessing the future demand for movement by road was to examine or count the then existing flows, and extrapolate these to some future date by applying an appropriate growth factor.

In 1953 a major break-through was achieved with the work of Robert MITCHELL and Chester RAPKIN of the University of Pennsylvania.[4] Following an analysis of movement and land-use data for Philadelphia, they expounded the thesis that different types of land use generate different and variable traffic flows. This approach brought about fundamental changes in the study and understanding of movement. It shifted the emphasis from the study of road traffic flows to the study of the land uses that give rise to the flows. It underlined the basic dictum that movement desires can be manipulated by controlling the land uses that represent the origins and destinations

15

of journeys. The approach was successfully applied in the *Detroit Area Traffic Study* (1953), the *Chicago Area Transportation Study* (1956), the *Penn-Jersey Transportation Study* and the *Tri-State New York Metropolitan Transportation Study*, and now dominates the large urban transportation studies supported by the U.S. Bureau of Public Roads. Indeed, to qualify for financial assistance in road construction, the 213 urban areas of over 50,000 population in the U.S.A. must, under the Federal Aid Highway Act 1962, carry out a continuing, comprehensive land-use/transportation study.

2 *Great Britain*

In Britain the interest in large-scale urban studies received a major impetus in the late fifties when the highway authorities in the major conurbations were encouraged by the Ministry of Transport to co-operate and produce long-term highway plans for their areas. This resulted in the setting up of teams comprised of local authority staff to carry out conurbation-wide studies, such as the *London Traffic Survey* (1960)[5] and that leading to the production of the *SELNEC Highway Plan* in 1962.[6] In the earlier studies, such as the *SELNEC Study*, the emphasis was placed on road traffic—data was collected at roadside interviews relating to vehicle movements; volumetric counts were taken and projected flows were estimated using growth factors. Later examples of the same type of study, such as the *Merseyside Conurbation Traffic Survey*,[7] developed the techniques used to include an examination of public transport movements. Projection of future movements was derived using differential growth factors based on population and car ownership.

The *London Traffic Survey*[8] was initiated in 1960 within this same framework, and its initial rather limited objectives were basically:

1 to survey the origins and destinations of traffic movements within an area extending beyond the boundaries of the then London County Council.

2 to survey journey times

3 to develop a method to estimate the amount of traffic on a road network

16

4 to indicate areas where travel capacity was limited, and travel conditions poor

5 to present the results in a form suitable for the preparation of a comprehensive road plan for the County of London

A firm of consultant engineers were appointed to develop the initial ideas into a working programme.

During the early stages of this study the significance of trends in transportation planning in U.S.A. was gradually realised and amended objectives, which included the estimation of future planning data, were incorporated in Phase II of the study.[9] Following the publication of the *Traffic in Towns Report*, establishing quite clearly the need for comprehensive movement studies involving land-use analysis, the Ministers of Transport and Housing and Local Government issued a joint circular in 1964 advocating the use of land-use transportation studies to achieve a co-ordinated approach to land use and transport planning.[10]

In April 1964 the Ministry of Transport, in conjunction with the local authorities concerned, commissioned the first of these land-use/transportation studies—the *West Midlands Transportation Study*. The objectives were:

'To undertake a comprehensive survey of all forms of transport in the West Midlands conurbation, and to analyse its relationship to types of land use and all other factors affecting the demand for and movement of transport; and to make forward projections with the aim of providing guidance on the desirable pattern of road development and public transport facilities.'[11]

Since the launching of this study other conurbation studies have been instigated. The most important development in study objectives since the *West Midlands Study* has been the recognition of the need to examine alternative land-use strategy plans for long-term development. Although the development of the plan for Cumbernauld New Town involved the examination of alternative land-use proposals, the *Teesside Study* is the first major study in Britain that can be described as a land-use/transportation study, and its primary aim is to produce an urban strategy plan for 1991.[12] Similar objectives have been adopted by the *Merseyside (1966)* and the *West Yorkshire Studies (1967)*.

Organisation and administration

Patterns of movement do not accord with administrative boundaries. To arrive at a realistic assessment of travel needs, it is necessary to include within the scope of the study all existing and planned developments which are oriented towards the main centre under examination. Thus the transportation study examining Glasgow's movement problem included within the study area towns such as Hamilton and Cumbernauld in the east, and Johnstone in the west. Similarly the *West Midlands Transportation Study* covered an area which included ten local authorities, and affected the interests of other bodies such as British Rail, the 'Midland Red' omnibus operators, and government departments. It is desirable that all these interests be represented in the organisation and administration of the study. Only in exceptional cases (e.g. *Belfast Transportation Study*) is one single local authority directly involved and this simplifies some of the organisational problems. In addition to the 'local' interests affected by the study, central government interests such as the Ministries of Transport and Housing and Local Government must also be represented. Experience has shown that possibly the most appropriate form of organisation for a transportation study which affects a multiplicity of different interests consists of a steering committee, a technical committee and the consultant engineer's representatives. Such a system was adopted in the *West Midlands Transportation Study* with some success, and is illustrated in Figure 1.

In the *West Midlands Study* the Steering Committee was formed of representatives of ten local authorities, the Ministries of Transport and Housing and Local Government, British Rail and the Midland Red Bus Company, and was responsible for: the setting up of the Technical Committee and the definition of its constitution; the retaining of the firm of consultant engineers; and for the decisions governing the financial contributions to be made by member bodies.

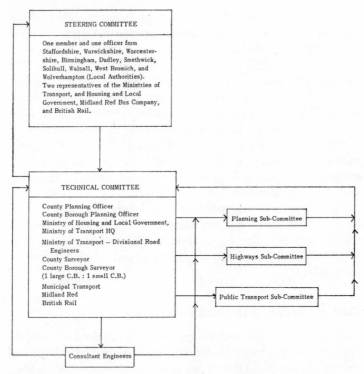

Fig. 1   Composition of the West Midlands Conurbation Transportation Study Organisation

SOURCE   Transportation Studies: A Review of Results to Date in Typical Areas, West Midlands Conurbation (Proceedings: Transportation Engineering Conference, April 1968), Institution of Civil Engineers.

The Technical Committee was designed with a view to ensuring that all interests were adequately represented by technically competent members, without producing a committee of unmanageable size. No attempt was made to give a full geographical representation. Rather, a group was established whereby the two Ministries and the other outside bodies concerned each had one representative, whilst one technical officer from different local authorities was appointed to represent a particular function, e.g. County Planning Officer, Borough Engineer.

19

Under the chairmanship of the appropriate member of the Technical Committee, sub-committees were set up to provide additional consultation wherever necessary. These sub-committees studied specific questions remitted to them by the Technical Committee, and produced reports on these matters.

The Consultant Engineers, under a study director, were responsible to the Technical Committee for the preparation of a project report outlining a programme of work (including estimates of the time and costs involved to meet the requirements of the brief), and for the conduct of the work which was carried out within a framework of shared technical direction and executive decision.

The success with which the many and varied interests affected by the *West Midlands Study* were co-ordinated to produce a transportation policy in so short a time reflects to no little extent the quality of the organisation and administration of the study.

Cost of transportation studies

Data collection and analysis on the scale required in comprehensive transportation studies is expensive of time, labour and money. At first sight the money required to finance such undertakings appears excessive, e.g. The *London Traffic Survey* is estimated to have cost £1m for the first three phases; the *West Midlands Study* cost £310,000; the *Merseyside Study* is estimated to have cost £420,000. However, it should be remembered that these undertakings comprise the necessary research work preliminary to the design and construction of transportation proposals, and, as such, the costs involved in the survey and analysis stage represent only a minor proportion of the total investment required to construct the proposed transport system (e.g. although the *London Traffic Survey* cost £1m this represents approximately 0·01% of the total investment required for roads that possibly might be constructed). In another way, the cost per head of population within the study area for the London Traffic Survey was approximately 2*s*. 10*d*. per head.

Transportation planning process in outline

Proposals resulting from the transportation planning process can take many different forms. Road improvements or traffic management schemes could result from a limited transportation study. Rail improvements, such as the electrification of the Euston–Manchester line and the reconstruction of Euston Station, could result from another form of transportation study, whilst new roads, such as the M1, could result from yet another form of transportation study. Such limited studies usually involve the consideration of only one mode of travel. Urban transportation studies on the other hand involve the consideration of several modes of travel, and their interactance one with another; and are consequently much more complex. However, all these different types of transportation study, although they are designed to meet different objectives, have the same basic framework. Each involves:

1 a survey and analysis stage which establishes the present demand for movement and how this is met, and the relationships between this demand for movement and the urban environment.

2 a prediction and plan formulation stage, which projects for some future date the likely travel demand—based on the data collected and the relationship established in the survey and analysis stage—and puts forward proposals to meet this demand.

3 an evaluation stage which attempts to assess whether the transportation proposals put forward satisfy the projected demand for travel with adequate safety, capacity and levels of service, and provide the maximum benefits to the community for minimum costs.

These three stages are an essential part of any transportation planning process. However, the urban transportation planning process, because of its complexity, is the most comprehensive example of the procedures and techniques involved. Consequently, to obtain as complete a picture as possible of the transportation planning process, it is essential that the urban transportation study be outlined in full. The more limited studies, with limited objectives, generally tend to consist of part of the overall urban process.

The urban transportation planning process is based on a set of principles and assumptions, the most basic of which is that travel patterns are tangible, stable and predictable. In addition to this fundamental assumption, it has been found necessary in the light of experience to assume that

1 decisive relationships exist between all modes of transport, and that the future rôle of a particular mode cannot be determined without giving consideration to all other modes.

2 the transportation system influences the development of an area, as well as serving that area.

3 areas of continuous urbanisation require a region-wide consideration of the transport situation.

4 the transportation study is an integral part of the overall planning process, and cannot adequately be considered in isolation.

5 the transportation planning process is continuous, and requires constant up-dating, validating and amendment.

Given these principles and assumptions it is evident that if transportation planning is to be effective it must be comprehensive and co-ordinated with other aspects of the overall planning process. It must therefore reflect the views of all the specialists involved in planning—the engineer, the traffic and transportation specialists, the town planner, and the economist—as well as meeting the requirements of the population at large. To achieve this, team-work of the highest order is required.

The principal steps involved in the urban transportation planning process can be readily identified as:

1 the collection of land-use, population, economic, and travel pattern data for the present-day situation.

2 the establishment of quantifiable relationships between present-day movements and the land-use, population and economic factors.

3 the prediction of land-use, population and economic factors to the target date for the study.

4 the prediction of the origins, destinations and distribution of the future movement demands, using the relationships established for the present-day situation and the predicted land-use, population and economic factors.

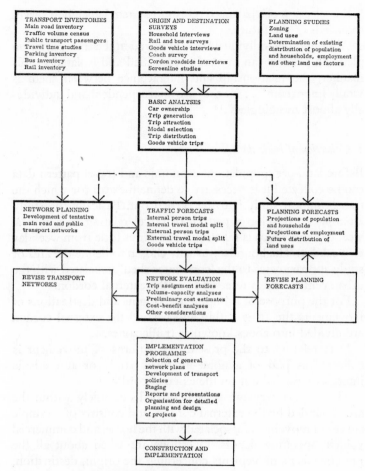

Fig. 2 The transportation planning process

SOURCE J. A. Proudlove. Some comments on the West Midlands Transport Study, Traffic Engineering and Control. November 1968.

5 the prediction of the person-movements likely to be carried by the different modes of travel at the target date.

6 the assignment of predicted trips to alternative co-ordinated transport systems.

7 the evaluation of the efficiency and economic viability of the alternative transport systems proposed.

8 the selection of a balanced transport system which best serves the needs of the future.

Although the individual steps involved in the transportation planning process can be readily identified and isolated in this manner, the relationship and interactance between them is vitally important '. . . for they are interdependent and individually almost meaningless'.[13]

1 *Collection of basic data*

Before land-use, population, economic and travel pattern data can be collected it is necessary to define the area for which the transportation study is to be carried out. Basically the study attempts to develop a pattern of travel relating to a typical weekday and which is repetitive, and varies little from weekday to weekday. The boundary usually chosen to define the area of study approximates to the 'commuter-shed' associated with the urban centre, and is referred to as the external cordon.

For the purpose of grouping the origins and destinations of movements the areas within and beyond the external cordon are divided into zones known as traffic zones.

Data relating to the present-day patterns of movement is collected as part of a home-interview study or at roadside interviews carried out on the external cordon.

The home-interview study is carried out solely within the area bounded by the external cordon, and consists of a sample survey of movements associated with the home, and commercial vehicle operating depots. Questions are asked about all the previous day's movements concerning the origin, destination, purpose and method of completing the journey.

The roadside interviews carried out at the external cordon are designed to collect data about movements originating outside the area of study, but which pass through the area of study or have a destination within the external cordon. Questions are asked about the origin, destination and purpose of the journey, and the mode of transport is noted by the interviewer.

Land-use, population and economic data relating to the present-day situation is collected for each zone of the survey, within the external cordon, and should provide zonal estimates of the total population, the employed population, the number of dwelling units, the number of motor vehicles, median household income, the number of jobs available, the volume of retail sales, school attendance and the area of land given over to different uses.

In addition to the planning and movement data, an inventory of the existing transport facilities must be carried out. This should include parking surveys, travel time surveys, and highway capacity and volume studies.

2 *Establishment of quantifiable relationships between movement and land use*

By using statistical techniques such as Multiple Linear Regression Analysis, relationships between the present-day patterns of movement and the land-use, population, and economic data are established. For a given area or traffic zone, the number of daily person trips produced by the residents of the area is correlated with such factors as population, population density, income and car ownership in a mathematical expression or formula. For the same area the number of daily person trips attracted to the zone is correlated with such factors as the number of jobs available, the volume of retail sales and school attendance. Again this relationship is expressed in the form of a mathematical formula or model.

3 *Prediction of future land-use, population and economic data*

Demands for movement are related to activities pursued by people, and these activities are reflected in the distribution and characteristics of a range of different land uses. Present-day demands for movement are related to existing land uses to establish quantifiable relationships. These relationships are then applied to future estimates of land-use distribution and characteristics to derive an estimate of future travel demands. The assumption that future land-use distribution and characteristics can be predicted accurately is fundamental to the transportation planning process, and for this stage, at least, the

25

traffic and transportation specialists are dependent on the skills and ability of the town planner. To allow the application of recognised transportation planning procedures it is necessary to have estimates, on a zonal basis and for some future date, of population, economic activity, vehicle ownership and land-use characteristics.

Population is fundamental in the provision of these estimates as it determines the growth in economic activity, the requirements for additional or new land uses, and the demands for future levels of transportation. It is important to estimate the total population growth of the area under study since future trip generation and distribution depend on this. In addition a knowledge of the location of this growth is equally important. In Britain, this latter aspect at least superficially presents few problems as the planning system allows for the control of the location and timing of development. Several well-tried techniques are available to predict future population growth, and it is not the purpose of this book to outline these techniques, which are well documented elsewhere.[14] However, it should be pointed out that such techniques are subject to uncertainty, although in the transportation planning process this can be partially overcome by planning for a certain level of population rather than for a specific date, and by adjusting the programme of construction accordingly. From estimated population growth it is possible to derive residential land-use requirements.

A forecast of future economic activity provides the basis for estimates of non-residential land use, and future trip-generation rates. It is essential that reliable estimates of employment be provided, and it is usual for these estimates to differentiate between extractive, manufacturing, and service industries. In addition, the changing requirements and productivity of the employment concerns must also be determined. Again, numerous techniques have been developed to predict future economic activity, including forecasts by Time Series, Correlation, Input–Output Analysis and the Economic Base Multiplier Method. However, these techniques will not be described here as they are beyond the scope of this work—they, too, are well documented elsewhere.[15] The per capita income likely to be enjoyed at some future date should also form part of the economic predictions, for increased income will result in more money being available to spend on 'non-essential' items such as recreation and travel, which will in turn influence the demand for travel.

Similarly, estimates should be derived for future levels of vehicle ownership. The bases for these forecasts are the population and economic activity forecasts used in conjunction with established trends in vehicle ownership. A variety of techniques have been established to derive future levels of vehicle ownership, but perhaps the most suitable method is the use of the logistic curve developed in Britain by TANNER.[16]

Forecasts of the distribution of future land uses must also provide estimates on a zonal basis of the resident and employed population. The principal factors influencing the distribution of land uses include topography, population, the availability of services such as drainage and transport, amenity considerations and the cost of development. In Britain the planning system is such that extensive controls are available to influence and restrict the development of land. Consequently, given the fact that it is possible to predict population and economic activity growth rates, it is generally assumed to be a reasonably straight-forward process to derive the distribution of land uses. However, enormous problems exist in attempting to predict future population and economic activity rates accurately, with the result that the very basis of transportation planning—i.e. forecasts of future land use, economic and population characteristics—as well as the other stages of the process are open to question. Indeed it could be argued that despite the imperfections inherent in the trip generation, trip distribution, traffic assignment and modal split stages of the process, these aspects are much more sophisticated, reliable and better understood than the techniques and methods used to forecast future land-use requirements in town planning today.

4 *Prediction of future origins, destinations and distribution of person movements*

This part of the procedure can be subdivided into two stages —a trip generation stage, and a trip distribution stage.

Trip generation can be defined as the determination of the number of trips associated with a traffic zone, area of land, or other unit of generation, and consists of trips produced by, and attracted to, the generation unit. These are referred to as trip productions and trip attractions.

Trip distribution is the allocation of a given number of trips between each pair of traffic zones, or unit of generation, in the study area.

To predict the number of trip productions and attractions associated with each traffic zone in the study area, it is necessary to utilise the mathematical relationships established between land use and patterns of movement for present-day conditions. On the assumption that these relationships will not alter materially in the future, the predicted land-use, population and economic data (e.g. population, numbers in employment) are substituted in the formula, and the equation is solved to derive the predicted trip productions and attractions for each traffic zone.

In the trip distribution stage of the process the number of trip productions and attractions estimated in the trip generation stage is used in conjunction with recognised mathematical techniques, to achieve a distribution of future trips between specific zones of origin and destination.

Two basic methods are used to achieve a satisfactory distribution of future trips—Growth Factor or Analogous Methods and Synthetic or Inter-Area Travel Formulae. The growth factor methods were the first to be developed for major use in trip distribution forecasts. They are simple to understand and use, and require little basic understanding of the underlying reasons as to why persons and traffic move. In general the growth factor methods calculate the future distribution of trips by multiplying the present-day pattern of movements by a growth factor, which can be derived in a variety of ways—usually from some combination of estimated total area or zonal growth rates. The most widely used growth factor methods are the Uniform Factor, the Average Factor, Fratar and Detroit Methods.

The Synthetic Methods used to predict future trip distribution vary widely in detail, but in general terms fall into four main categories—the Gravity Models, the Opportunity Models, the Electrostatic Field Model and the Multiple Linear Regression Models.

The Gravity Model as applied in transportation planning is based on Newton's Law of Gravity and assumes that all trips originating in a particular zone will distribute themselves amongst all other zones in accordance with the attractiveness of the competing destinations (usually indicated by some measure of size such as the total number of jobs available within the destination) and in inverse proportion to a measure of the travel resistance between the zones (typical measures of travel resistance are distance, and journey time).

In mathematical terms the Gravity Model is expressed:

$$T_{i-j} = \frac{P_i \dfrac{A_j}{(D_{i-j})^b}}{\dfrac{A_j}{(D_{i-j})^b} + \dfrac{A_k}{(D_{i-k})^b} + \ldots\ldots + \dfrac{A_n}{(D_{i-n})^b}}$$

where T_{i-j} = number of trips produced in zone i with a destination in zone j.

P_i = total number of trips produced in zone i.

$A_j \ldots A_n$ = total number of trips attracted to zone $j \ldots {}_n$.

$D_{i-j} \ldots D_{i-n}$ = measure of spatial separation between zones $i-j$ and $i-n$.

b = empirically determined exponent which expresses the average area wide effect of spatial separation between zones on trip interchange.

It should be pointed out that the measures of attraction and travel resistance used vary with trip purpose, e.g. people are generally prepared to travel much further to work than to shop. Consequently the Gravity Model is used to distribute trips stratified by different purposes, rather than to distribute total trips.

Opportunity models were first developed and used on the *Chicago*, and the *Pittsburgh Area Transportation Studies*, and use the theory of probability in deriving estimates of future trip distribution. Basically these models assume that the probability that a trip will go to a particular destination depends on the relationship between the opportunities for satisfying a trip in the destination area and the other opportunities acting in competition with the chosen destination zone. Thus the attracting power of a zone of destination is conditioned by the number of trip opportunities in that zone (such as the total number of jobs) and by the number of trip opportunities within the same time or distance from the zone of origin.

The 'Electrostatic Field' Method of trip distribution was developed in an attempt to eliminate the need for expensive home-interview studies. It is based on Coulomb's Law of Electrostatic Force, and assumes that movement occurs within a system because of an initial imbalance between the number of jobs (which are regarded as positive charges) and the number of people looking for employment (which are regarded as negative charges). However, the model is similar in form to the gravity Model, and although it has been tested in research projects has not been widely used in transportation studies.

The Multiple Linear Regression Model is an empirical attempt to determine the distribution of future trips from the mathematical relationship which exists between present-day trip distribution and land use and socio-economic character-istics of the population. Using this relationship and predicting the future land use and socio-economic characteristics the future number of trips between pairs of zones can be estimated.

This method of trip distribution is easily understood, and has the advantage that any variable thought to influence trip distribution can be included in the basic relationship. However, the method is expensive of computer time and for this reason has not been widely used in transportation studies.

5 *Estimation of future person movements carried by different modes of travel*

The estimation of the future person movements likely to be carried by different modes of travel can occur at different stages in the transportation planning process. It can be introduced at the trip generation stage when estimates of person movements made by different modes of travel are derived, in addition

30

to the total person movements generated. Alternatively the future modal split can be estimated at or before the traffic assignment stage and after the trip distribution stage, when the appropriate proportions of the total person movements are allocated to the different modes of travel such as public transport and the private motor vehicle.

Considerable work has been carried out on the modal split stage of the process, and it is generally understood that factors such as income, the availability and convenience of alternative modes of transport, and length of journey all affect an individual's choice of mode of transport for a particular journey. However, these relationships are only imperfectly understood, and much more research into the motivation behind people's choice of transport mode is necessary before the modal split stage of the process can be applied with any confidence.

6 *Assignment of future trips to the proposed transport networks*

From an analysis of the distances and journey times on each section of the different transport systems in the area under study it is possible to estimate the routes most likely to be taken between each pair of zones. Total person or vehicular movements derived at the trip distribution stage can then be assigned to these routes.

A variety of assignment techniques have been developed in the past decade, the most significant of which are the Diversion Curve, 'All or Nothing' and 'Capacity Restraint' assignment procedures.

The Diversion Curve was the first assignment technique to be developed. It is based on empirical studies and in general terms estimates the proportion of persons or vehicles likely to transfer to a new or improved facility. The proportion of diverted traffic is generally related to such parameters as distance, cost, or speed.

The All or Nothing assignment is based on the assumption that all movements between each pair of zones will take the shortest route between the zones. All the trip interchanges between zones derived from the trip distribution stages are allocated to this shortest route, and the total traffic volumes on each section (or link) of the system are then summed to estimate the traffic volumes assigned to the network. The most recently developed traffic assignment technique is the Capacity Restraint assignment. This technique is similar to the All or Nothing assignment in the early stages, in that movements between each pair of zones are assigned to the shortest route. However, in an attempt to simulate the real-life situation, this technique also takes account of the congestion which builds up with increased traffic volumes, and as the capacity of each section of the transport networks are reached, so movements are assigned to the next shortest route.

7 *Evaluation of efficiency and economic viability of alternative schemes*

The evaluation stage of the transportation planning process is probably the most important stage, which as yet is only imperfectly understood and often ignored except for initial, intuitive judgements. On the traffic side, and within the limitation imposed by the numerous assumptions made in the process, it is a comparatively straight-forward matter to assess whether the proposed transport networks fulfil the estimated travel demand with adequate capacity, safety, and standard of service. However, the problems associated with the assessment of the economics of alternative proposals are considerable. Although the cost of implementing and operating transport proposals can be estimated reasonably adequately, the price mechanism cannot be used as an investment criterion as 'vehicle-miles' is not a commodity which is directly bought and sold. In addition many of the benefits derived from a particular proposal are 'social' benefits and as such cannot be valued.

In an attempt to overcome these problems a technique known as Cost-Benefit Analysis has been developed to guide investment. In theory, the application of this technique is a comparatively simple exercise in which costs (including capital, operating and maintenance costs) and benefits (including savings in time, accidents and operating costs) are assessed for future years and discounted back to the base year, so that a rate of return on the investment might be calculated. In practice, however, it is extremely difficult to apply this technique except in a most general way, because of the problems associated with the assumption of values for future savings and costs, and for social and environmental costs and benefits.

Evaluation techniques are now receiving considerable research attention, and with time should become more sophisticated and reliable. Even today, however, and despite the crude approaches adopted, evaluation of alternative proposals should be undertaken as an integral part of the transportation planning process. If nothing else, the use of such techniques attempts to rationalise the investment decision-making process.

8 The selection of a balanced transport system

The decision as to which transport system best serves the needs of the community cannot be made by the transportation planning process. Future traffic estimation is an important and powerful tool which can only be used to rationalise the decision-making process, and to help man make decisions which are sound and logical rather than intuitive. It is important to realise that the transportation planning process is no more than this. The often sweeping assumptions which are fundamental to the different stages of the process, and the lack of knowledge concerning the prediction of future land uses ensure that accurate results are impossible except by coincidence. But, equally important, accuracy for its own sake is valueless since forecasts to the nearest traffic lane width are all that are required. The transportation planning process is basically an aid to orderly decision making, and not the precise instrument that some people like to think it is.

A further problem which must be faced in selecting the most appropriate form of transport system, is to ensure that any proposals put forward are not so rigid as to prejudice the course of progress. In the last half-century change has been occurring at a tremendous rate—in the technological field advances in transportation have been enormous; demographically changes in family size, age of marriage, size of the working population and its age and sex structure make it impossible to predict accurately population trends for more than 5–10 years ahead; economic advances have led directly to changes in the pattern of industrial growth and indirectly to changes in the skills, demands and standards of the employees.

Changes of this sort can be equated with progress, and it is important that plans are flexible enough to accommodate any changes brought about by progress. Flexibility can be achieved by presenting the range of long-term possibilities that might develop out of the present situation, and ensuring that by picking a path common to the range in the short term, nothing, is done to prejudice these possibilities. However, no plan can have infinite flexibility for decisions have to be taken in the light of the best advice and information available at the time. In the words of the *South Hampshire Study*:

> 'Planning . . . is becoming less and less a matter of precise propositions committed to paper and more and more a matter of ideas and policies loosely assembled under constant review, within which, every now and then, some project is seen to be as ready for execution as human judgement can pronounce.'[17]

In transportation planning this 'constant review' is part of the process. Although policies are laid out for the long term, projections are also made for the short term (5 years) and interim periods (up to 10–15 years). Checks are made against these short-term projections by actually observing what happens at those dates and comparing them with the projected trends. If the comparisons are good, then no changes to the policies are made. If comparisons are bad, then the assumptions made at the outset could well have been wrong and must be reviewed and up-dated.

References

1 Buchanan C. D., *Traffic in Towns—Reports of the Steering Group and Working Group*, Para. 55, H.M.S.O. London (1963).
2 Dykeman J. W., Transport in cities, *Scientific American*. (1965).
3 *Traffic in Towns*, *op. cit.*, Para. 59.

4 Mitchell R. and Rapkin C., *Urban Traffic—A Function of Land Use*, Columbia University Press (1954).

5 *The London Traffic Survey*: Volume 1, The London County Council, London (1964).

6 *SELNEC: A highway plan 1962*, prepared by the South-East Lancashire and North-East Cheshire Highway Engineering Committee (1962).

7 *Merseyside Conurbation Traffic Survey 1962*, prepared by the Steering Committee on Merseyside Traffic and Transport (1965).

8 *The London Traffic Survey, op. cit.*

9 *The London Traffic Survey*, Volume 2, The Greater London Council, London, July (1966).

10 Ministry of Transport and Ministry of Housing and Local Government, Circular 1/64; *Buchanan Report, Traffic in Towns*, H.M.S.O. London (1964).

11 Freeman, Fox, Wilbur Smith and Associates, *The West Midlands Transport Study* (1968).

12 Spence R., Transportation studies: a review of results to date from typical areas and a critical assessment, *Proceedings of the Transportation Engineering Conference*, organised by the Institution of Civil Engineers, London (1968).

13 Davinroy T. R., Ridley T. M. and Wootton H. J., Predicting future travel, *Traffic Engineering and Control* (1963).

14 Barclay G. W., *Techniques of Population Analysis*, Wiley, New York (1958).

15 *The Role of Economic Studies in Urban Transportation Planning*; Urban Planning Division, Bureau of Public Roads, Washington (1965).

16 Tanner J. C., Forecasts of Future Numbers of Vehicles in Great Britain, *Roads and Road Construction* (1962).

17 Buchanan Colin and Partners, *South Hampshire Study*, H.M.S.O. London (1966).

2 Collection of basic data

Introduction

The transportation planning process involves the accumulation of a considerable amount of basic data. Characteristics of the present-day travel pattern in the area under consideration must be collected, the future distribution of land use and population derived, the adequacy or otherwise of existing transportation facilities determined and any spare capacity estimated. Although the amount of basic data collected, and the detail in which it is presented, varies according to the purpose of the study and the size of the area under consideration, the principles governing the gathering of this data are broadly similar.

The different surveys necessary to collect the basic data are time-consuming and expensive of both staff and money. Consequently careful programming of this collection process is required, and it is now standard practice to analyse each element in the process, allocate an estimate of the time necessary to complete each element and from this data prepare a critical path diagram, to ensure that the required data is assembled as quickly and efficiently as possible.

Definition of study area

To ensure that all travel-pattern and land-use data relating to the transportation planning process is collected in an efficient

36

and economic manner the area to be studied is defined by a boundary known as an external cordon. Basically, the area within the external cordon is surveyed intensively—present and future land uses are analysed in some detail and travel-pattern data is assembled by means of a 'home-interview' study. Movements originating outside the external cordon, but crossing the cordon, are surveyed at the point at which they cross it.

Outside the external cordon changes in the land-use pattern are considered to be less significant, and therefore are examined in a less detailed manner. No home-interview studies are carried out beyond the external cordon.

In defining the study area, three main criteria must be met:

1 The external cordon should isolate those problems of movement which are crucial to the daily life of the urban centre being studied. To achieve this, it should circumscribe the zone of systematic daily movement oriented towards the urban centre. Generally, this means that sub-urban and semi-rural areas which generate a regular flow of trips, especially work trips, to the urban centre are included within the study area. Details of these movements are most easily surveyed by a home-interview study. Those residents who live further out make fewer trips to the urban centre, with the result that there comes a point when it is easier and more economic to survey these movements at a roadside interview rather than use a home-interview study. External cordons therefore tend to be drawn at the 'commuter-sheds' between urban areas.

2 the external cordon should include the area into which future urban development will probably extend during the period for which the transportation facilities are to be planned.

3 the external cordon should meet certain technical requirements for roadside interviewing of traffic, viz. to reduce the number of survey points at the cordon, the cordon line should be located in the fringe area of the urban region where movements are channelled on to a reasonably small number of roads. It should cross roads at a point where it is safe to carry out roadside interviews; it should be continuous, and it should be uniform in its course so that movements (with the exception of movements passing through the area) cross it only once.

A recent interesting development in the process of defining

the external cordon has been the use of census data by the *Tri-State New York Metropolitan Transportation Study* to determine the extent of urbanisation. On the basis that the external cordon should include all continuous urban development, as well as the expected future population increase, the Tri-State Study determined the extent of urbanisation by plotting population density and car ownership per acre for each municipality. This gave a good indication of population dispersion from high intense urbanisation to surburban and then rural conditions, and provided a visual idea of the area which should be encompassed by the cordon. Alternative cordon lines derived from this exercise were tested with 'pilot' roadside interviews, and the broad effect of future land-use changes within these cordon lines evaluated. Finally, the most suitable cordon line was chosen.[1]

For free-standing towns this method would appear to have little advantage over the more traditional approach as outlined above. However, in the more complex built-up areas of the conurbations this method might well be used with advantage.

Subdivision of area into traffic zones

The objectives of the survey and analysis stage of the tranportation planning process are to
1 determine where journeys begin and end
2 determine the factors which influence trip generation
3 establish the main 'corridors of movement'.

However, the mass of data collected relates to individual journeys, households and centres of employment, and in its crude form is difficult to analyse and interpret. To overcome this problem the area being surveyed, and indeed the whole country, is divided into zones, for the purpose of ' . . . (grouping) the data so as to make it intelligible, amenable to analysis, and suitable for the assignment of journeys . . .'.[2] The procedure is similar to choosing class intervals for a histogram—intervals which do not oversimplify the data, but which bring some order to it.

To ensure that information is collected in sufficient detail to enable meaningful conclusions to be drawn about trip generation rates, and trip distribution, two main types of traffic zone are distinguished:

1 External zones—that is traffic zones outside the external cordon boundary.

2 Internal zones—that is zones contained within the external cordon. These zones are further subdivided into central area zones, and non-central area zones.

1 *External zones*

The traffic zones defined beyond the external cordon cover the whole country. As the influence of traffic generators tends to decrease with distance away from the study area, so the size of external traffic zones is increased with distance from the study area. In these outer areas population centres, the communications network, and topographical features must all be taken account of in defining the external zone boundaries, but the basic principle to be followed is that those centres of population close enough to the study area to generate significant traffic flows to that area, should be separately zoned.

In Great Britain, the Ministry of Transport has prepared a standard system of defining external zones for transportation studies, which tends to be adopted in those studies which are financed in part by the Government.[3]

2 *Internal zones*

For internal traffic within the study area the aim is to define zones small enough to give accuracy of movement, and to allow reliable trip generation rates to be established. This is normally achieved by dividing the area bounded by the external cordon into sectors one of which is the central area. The other sectors are defined working outwards from the central area and using topographical barriers, such as rivers, canals, railways, in conjunction with natural traffic catchment areas, to delineate boundaries.[4]

The sectors are then further subdivided into zones and sub-zones, on the basis of the predominant land use, e.g. residential, shopping, recreational, industrial. The zonal boundaries used by other bodies for the collection of information related to the travel pattern data must be taken into consideration if it is to be used in the analysis stage of the transportation planning process.

Traffic movement will certainly be related to population. Therefore it is always advisable to relate these zones as far as possible to Enumeration District boundaries.

Land-use data collected by the Local Planning Authority is often processed for street blocks or units, and if it is intended to relate traffic movement to land-use or floor-space characteristics, then the street block boundaries should be taken into consideration when defining traffic zones.

Employment data relating to firms employing five persons or more is available from the Ministry of Labour for Employment Exchange areas and Employment Districts within the Exchange area. If this is to be used in conjunction with travel pattern data then the boundaries of these areas must be taken account of when drawing up traffic zones.

In addition to considering land use, population and employment 'zone' boundaries when drawing up traffic zones, the more recent transportation studies also take account of environmental areas and groupings.

The size of traffic zone required varies with the different stages of the transportation planning process. The zones required for the establishment of trip generation rates are generally smaller than those required for trip distribution. This is largely because to establish reliable trip generation rates it is necessary for the particular land use to exhibit similar characteristics, so that it might reasonably be assumed that the traffic generation rate is also similar. Thus as far as possible households of similar types will be grouped together—owner-occupied properties, at a low density of development are not as a rule grouped with high density council-rented property. This principle is applied to other land uses.

Trip distribution, which simulates travel patterns in a general way, often requires larger zones because of the comparatively small amount of travel pattern data relating to the trip generation zones. It is usually found necessary to combine these smaller trip generation zones to derive a reliable distribution of trips.

40

The size of zones required for the trip assignment stage of the process will vary with the computer programme used. However, the zones chosen for trip generation are invariably satisfactory, and for assignment purposes these are either used as they stand or are aggregated to form larger more suitable zones.

The capacity of the computer available to analyse the data will often prove to be the limiting factor in the number, and therefore the size, of the traffic zones to be used.

3 Central area zones

The definition of zones within the central area sector is based on the same procedure as that adopted for the internal zones. Factors of especial importance here are land use, and the Local Planning Authorities street block method of recording floor-space statistics for the various land uses.

4 Coding

If the transportation study is to be analysed by computer then the zoning and coding of the area tends to follow a standard pattern, to simplify the coding and data punching procedures. The external zones are usually prefixed by the digit 9. The area within the external cordon is normally sub-divided into nine sectors, one being the central area, which is given the prefix 0. The remaining eight sectors are then given the prefixes 1–8 numbering clockwise and outwards from the central area. The sectors are then subdivided into 10 zones numbered 0–9 using land-use and traffic catchment areas as guide lines, and if necessary these zones can be further divided into 10 sub-zones numbered 0–9, numbering outwards from the central area. Thus the reference 481 can be immediately recognised as Sector 4, zone 8, Sub-zone 1.

The central area, with the prefix 0, can similarly be divided into 10 zones numbered 0–9, and based on the predominant land use. Further division into sub-zones can be carried out if necessary.

Zones defined in this manner are usually plotted on maps of

different scale depending on the type of zones. It is normal practice for central-area zones to be plotted at 1:2500 or even 1:1250 scale. Internal zones are usually plotted at a 6-inch to 1-mile scale, although if the selection of the sample of households to be interviewed is based on a map of the internal zones, then they are plotted at 1:2500 scale. External zones are plotted at the scale of 10 miles to 1 inch.

Zoning by National Grid references

Traffic zones defined in the conventional method outlined above depend almost entirely on the judgement of the engineer, since they are defined without knowing the full facts necessary to draw a balance between conflicting requirements. In addition the need to index and code by zone number all place names likely to occur as origins or destinations, is a costly and time-consuming process. But perhaps the most significant disadvantage is the inability to alter zone boundaries after the preliminary analysis, without recoding all the place names in the data.

Because of these disadvantages associated with the conventional method of zoning for traffic surveys, attempts have been made in recent years to develop alternative techniques. In 1963 Worcestershire County Council, after consulting with the Ministry of Transport and the Road Research Laboratory, successfully carried out two Origin and Destination Surveys using National Grid Reference Numbers to define traffic zone boundaries.[5]

Basically the procedure adopted involved:

1 coding of all place names in the survey area by the grid reference listed in the Ordnance Survey Gazetteer.

2 preliminary computer analysis of

  a all journeys originating within each 1 km², within an area extending just beyond the County boundary.

  b all journeys originating within each 10 km² surrounding the County, and within an area measuring 300 km by 200 km on its outer boundary.

  c all journeys originating within each 100 km² for the remainder of Great Britain.

3 defining zone boundaries, around groups of squares using as guide lines the approximate optimum number of origins for each zone that experience in other surveys had shown was desirable, and other factors such as administrative boundaries, and the road network.

Because of the problems associated with manually specifying curvilinear boundaries, all zones in the two surveys conducted were straight lines.

The zone boundaries were specified for computer input by listing against each zone number the grid reference for every change of direction going in clockwise order round the zone.

4 traditional distribution of origins and destinations to the zones was then carried out by the computer, and normal journey analyses undertaken. The main operational advantages claimed for this method of zoning are:

'*a* Zoning can be related to the actual location and density of journey origins as disclosed by the survey.

b Errors in the coding of place names are minimised by reducing the task to its simplest possible form . . .

c Zoning can subsequently be changed without the need to recode the place names in the original data.'

In addition the adoption of this method on a wider basis would enable the results of different surveys carried out by different authorities to be collated and combined to make up a regional survey. It would also facilitate the accumulation and use of basic travel data for research purposes.

Travel pattern data

Travel pattern data is required for four basic movements.

1 External-External (or 'Through' movements) with an origin and a destination outside the area defined by the external cordon. Depending on the purpose of the study these movements are sometimes subdivided into

(*a*) through movements stopping in the town or area defined by the external cordon, and (*b*) non-stop through movements.

2 External-Internal Movements, with an origin outside the external cordon, and a destination within the cordon.

43

3 Internal-External Movements, which originate within the area defined by the external cordon, and have a destination beyond it.

4 Internal Movements with both their origin and destination inside the area bounded by the external cordon.

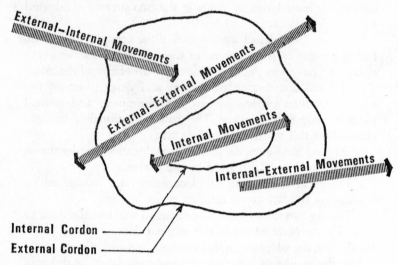

Internal Cordon ————
External Cordon ————

Fig. 3   Diagrammatic representation of the four basic movements for which data is collected in the transportation planning process

All these types of movement can be made by different modes and depending upon the purpose of the study this movement data may be collected for private motor vehicles, public transport, commercial vehicles, and even walking. For example, the transportation studies being undertaken in the conurbations of this country, which are designed to produce a plan for a 'primary' communications network, collected comprehensive movement data for all the above major modes. On the other hand, a limited transportation study carried out to determine whether or not a by-pass is required to a small country town, would be concerned primarily with the movements made by private motor vehicle.

Data relating to these different types of movement, is

collected in a variety of ways. Through movements, and External-Internal Movements are invariably surveyed at the external cordon. They are also picked up on an internal cordon or screen line survey, if this is considered necessary.

Internal-External Movements are surveyed in the home-interview study, if this is carried out, and are also picked up on the internal and external cordon surveys.

Movements occurring within the area defined by the external cordon are surveyed in the home-interview study. In addition an internal cordon or screen line survey is sometimes carried out as a check against the results of the home-interview and external cordon surveys.

The home-interview study

The home-interview study is concerned with the collection of basic facts relating to present-day movements for all trips on a typical day within the town or urban region defined by the external cordon. The survey includes home interviews, commercial vehicle and public transport surveys to determine movements originating within the area. Roadside interviews are carried out on the external cordon line to cover trips passing through or into the area.

These surveys provide the essential facts on present-day travel desires and habits, and in combination with data from land-use and economic studies serve as a basis for projecting future travel patterns.

1 *Home interview—sample size*

'Travel is an expression of an individual's behaviour, and as such it has the characteristics of being habitual. As a habit it tends to be repetitive and the repetition occurs in a definite pattern. In addition, travel habits of different individuals ... are similar for work, shopping, recreation and other types of trips.'[6]

Because patterns of movement exhibit these characteristics it is not necessary to obtain travel information from all

45

residents of the area under study, for a long period of time. Statistical methods can be used with confidence for the sampling of movement in urban areas.

To ensure that a sample is representative it is necessary that the persons included in it are distributed geographically throughout the survey area in the same proportion as the distribution of the total population. Experience has shown that the dwelling unit is the most reliable and convenient sampling unit to be used in home-interview studies.

The size of sample to be interviewed depends upon the total population of the area under study, the degree of accuracy required, and occasionally, on the density of population, e.g. a small town of primarily low density residential development will require a larger sample than a large, densely populated town. The adequacy of various sample sizes has been tested, and this has led to recommended sample sizes related to the population of the area under study.

Table 1. *Recommended sample sizes to be adopted in home-interview studies*

Population of area	Recommended sample size	Minimum sample size (dwelling units)
Under 50,000	1 in 5	1 in 10
50,000–150,000	1 in 8	1 in 20
150,000–300,000	1 in 10	1 in 35
300,000–500,000	1 in 15	1 in 50
500,000–1,000,000	1 in 20	1 in 70
Over 1,000,000	1 in 25	1 in 100

If the purpose of the study is to determine long term proposals then the minimum sample size is used. If a greater degree of reliability and accuracy is required then the recommended sample size is used.

The *Greater Glasgow Transportation Study* used a 1 in 30 sample for the home-interview study.

2 Home interview—selection of sample

The frame from which the sample of households is selected,

can be set up from either the electoral roll, or the rating lists. The electoral roll (or Register of Electors) is compiled annually and includes a list of the names and addresses of those persons who are qualified electors. It does not include any addresses at which all residents are under twenty-one years of age, or alien.

The rating (or Valuation Lists) which are compiled by the inland revenue and held by local authorities, comprise a list of all separately rated units, including those occupied by aliens and persons under twenty-one years. Although rateable units contained in the rating register tend to identify quite closely with individual households, there are problems associated with its use as a sample frame, e.g. buildings used for other than residential purposes, such as shops, offices, public buildings, are included in the register, amongst the dwelling unit records. Consequently these 'non-dwellings' must be eliminated before the sample of households is derived. A further administrative problem occurs when the study area includes several local authorities. This can be overcome by conducting primary sampling at the offices of the local authorities concerned. Unless great inconvenience is experienced in gaining access to the Valuation Lists it is recommended that they be used for the sample selection of households for home interview.[7]

The sample of residential buildings not occupied as single family dwelling units, such as hotels, institutions, and boarding houses, can usually be derived from the Valuation List. However, in those cases where it is difficult to determine the number of rooms or dwelling units in such buildings then the procedure adopted for sample selection is somewhat different. Whenever an hotel, or institution or boarding house is encountered in the Valuation List it is omitted from the sample frame. A separate record of its particulars, including location, is made, and on a subsequent date, often near the completion of the home-interview study, the number of 'dwellings' or rooms in each such building is determined by a field inspection. The actual sample to be interviewed is derived from this.

3 *Home interview—interview procedure*

Once the selection of the dwelling unit sample is completed,

Fig. 4 (Overleaf) Typical home-interview study form

WYCOMBE AREA TRANSPORTATION STUDY
HOME INTERVIEW SURVEY – PART 2

Zone........ Code No........ Page........of........

CODING COMPLETE	Card type
	Traffic zone
CODING CHECKED	Code No.
	Expansion factor
	Seasonal factor

PERSON INFORMATION

Person No.	Person identification	Journeys made	Direct interview	Sex	Age	Employment	Normal place of employment	Type of employment	Regular train travel — Departure station
		YES	YES	Male	Over 21	1 Full time	1 High Wycombe	1 Industry	1 High Wycombe
					Under 21 (state age)	2 Part time	2 Remainder Study area		2 Beaconsfield
		NO	NO	Female		3 Unemployed	3 Slough	5 Offices (state business of firm)	3 Great Missenden
						4 School or college	4 Beaconsfield		4 Amersham
						5 Housewife	5 Marlow	8 Shops	5 Saunderton
						6 Retired	6 Wooburn, Bourne End.	9 Other (state)	6 Other station
						7 Pre-school age	7 Greater London		7 None
							8 Elsewhere		

SURVEY DAY   SURVEY DATE

JOURNEY INFORMATION

Journey No.	ORIGIN Precise address if in Study Area	DESTINATION Precise address if in Study Area	TIME Start	TIME Finish	JOURNEY PURPOSE Ring appropriate letters From	JOURNEY PURPOSE Ring appropriate letters To	MODE OF TRAVEL Ring appropriate number	TRIP TYPE
			A.M.	A.M.	A Work	A Work	1 Drove car, light van	
					B School or college	B School or college	2 Drove goods vehicle	
			P.M.	P.M.	C In course of work	C In course of work	3 M/C, Scooter, moped	
					D Shopping personal business	D Shopping personal business	4 Rode pedal cycle	
					E Social sport, entertainment	E Social sport, entertainment	5 Passenger in car, van, taxi	
					F Serve passenger	F Serve passenger	6 Private coach or bus	
					G Home		7 Public service bus. coach	
					H Change mode		8 Train	
							9 Walk or other	
			A.M.	A.M.	A Work	A Work	1 Drove car, light van	
					B School or college	B School or college	2 Drove goods vehicle	
			P.M.	P.M.	C In course of work	C In course of work	3 M/C, Scooter, moped	
					D Shopping personal business	D Shopping personal business	4 Rode pedal cycle	
					E Social sport, entertainment	E Social sport, entertainment	5 Passenger in car, van, taxi	
					F Serve passenger	F Serve passenger	6 Private coach or bus	

Study Area:

High Wycombe	Bryant's Bottom	Great Kingshill	Lane End	Piddington	West Wycombe
Beamond End	Cryers Hill	Hazlemere	Loudwater	Terriers	Widmer End
Bolter End	Downley	Heath End	Lower North Dean	Tylers Green	Wooburn Green
Booker	Fingest	Holmer Green	Naphill	Upper North Dean	
Bradenham	Flackwell Heath	Hughenden	Penn	Walter's Ash	

Journey purpose:
- A Work
- B School or college
- C In course of work
- D Shopping personal business
- E Social sport, entertainment
- F Serve passenger
- G Home
- H Change mode

Mode:
- 1 Drove car, light van
- 2 Drove goods vehicle
- 3 M/C, Scooter, moped
- 4 Rode pedal cycle
- 5 Passenger in car, van, taxi
- 6 Private coach or bus
- 7 Public service bus, coach
- 8 Train
- 9 Walk or other

A.M.   P.M.

then the collection of data relating to internally generated movements can commence. Specially trained field interviewers, under the close guidance of a supervisor, are used for this purpose. They are given a list of addresses at which they are to call on a particular day. Three or four days before the intended visit a letter is sent to the householder explaining the reasons for the survey, and warning him that the interviewer will call on the appropriate day.

The information requested by the field interviewer covers basic household characteristics, and all the journeys made by each member of the household of five years of age and above in the previous twenty-four hours. This data is recorded on the home-interview form, a typical example of which is illustrated in Figure 4.

Basically, the household information gathered includes the address of the dwelling unit, the size of the household, and the age and sex structure of the occupants; the numbers economically active, their job, and place of work; the number of motor vehicles owned; the household income; the place of school/further education for those occupants of school age; and the day and date of the journeys to be reported, i.e. normally the previous day and date.

Often questions concerning income are omitted because of the reluctance of people to answer reliably such personal questions. However, an assessment of the household income can be derived from an analysis of the number of vehicles owned, the type of dwelling occupied, and the job of each employed member of the household. In these cases additional questions are asked about whether the property is owner-occupied, council-rented, or privately rented.

The information required from each member of the household of five years of age or more, about *all* the journeys made in the previous twenty-four hours includes the precise address of the origin and destination, the time of the start and finish of the journey, the purpose of the journey, and the mode of travel. Up to ten different journey purposes are distinguished, the most significant being to or from work, school or college, in course of work (including employer's business), social, sport or entertainment, serve passenger, home and change mode.

The most significant modes of travel distinguished are car driver, car passenger, goods vehicle driver, goods vehicle passenger, motor cycle/scooter, rail, bus, coach, taxi, pedal cycle and walk. Depending on the nature of the study some of these modes may be amalgamated or even omitted.

If the field interviewer cannot make contact with the householder on the appointed day, then he or she should call back on the following day. If no contact is made on the second visit, then no further attempt is made to contact the occupants until seven days after the appointed day.

Cordon surveys—external

The only satisfactory method of determining the origin and destination of through movements, and external–internal movements across the external cordon, is to question the persons actually making the movement. In transportation studies this is normally done by direct interview, or issuing pre-paid business reply postcards at the roadside.

Other methods, relying on the observation and identification of each movement across the cordon line, are sometimes used. However, the reliability of 'match registration', and 'tag and disc' surveys in anything but the smallest area leaves much to be desired, whilst the fundamental disadvantages of an incomplete knowledge of origin and destination cannot be overcome. Consequently direct interview or pre-paid postcard surveys tend to be favoured.

Road traffic movement   (a) postcard surveys

Pre-paid business reply postcards, with return address and questionnaire to be filled in by the road user, are distributed at the external cordon survey point. They are usually accompanied by a request for co-operation, the location of origin and destination, purpose of trips, and type of vehicle. The time, location and direction of travel are entered on the cards by the staff operating the survey, as they are distributed to the road users.

This method requires few enumerators, and site organisation, and delays to traffic are kept to a minimum. However, the response rate to such surveys is variable, and usually ranges from 10 to 50% of those issued with the postcards. In addition there is a danger that the 'returns' received form a biased sample. Experience in the United States of America shows that lower percentage returns are usual for commercial traffic, and night drivers, whilst drivers making more than one trip through the cordon are often reluctant to complete and return more than one card.

Nevertheless postcard surveys can be reasonably successfully utilised in heavy traffic conditions, pilot surveys, and where they are used in conjunction with some direct interviewing. They can also be successfully utilised in major transportation studies. as the experience of Buchanan and Partners with the *Bath Study* shows—a 72% return was achieved, but only after extensive and repeated publicity was given to the importance of the study in the local press.[8]

Road traffic movement   (b) direct interview

In the direct interview method, a sample of road users are stopped at the external cordon survey point, and questioned by an interviewer, who records the answers on specially prepared forms. Figure 5 illustrates a typical cordon survey form. The information recorded includes general information about the date, time, location of the survey point and the identification of the interviewer. The class of vehicle being interviewed is identified and entered on the form in code, as is the number of occupants in the vehicle. This information is normally recorded as the vehicle approaches the survey point.

Questions are then put to the driver of the vehicle about the origin and destination of his journey. Because the study area is divided into zones for the purposes of a transportation study all origins and destinations within the external cordon must be recorded in detail (e.g. street name and number, or the name of a well-known shop or firm). For points outside the study area, the name of the town or village, and the county is normally sufficient. The origin and destination of a trip must never be recorded as the same point. For round trips the farthest point

Fig. 5   Typical external cordon interview form

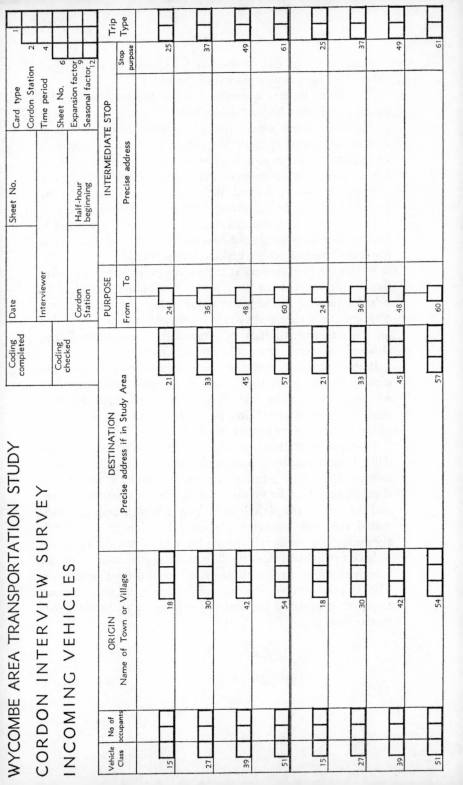

WYCOMBE AREA TRANSPORTATION STUDY
CORDON INTERVIEW SURVEY
INCOMING VEHICLES

reached from one end of the journey should be recorded as either the origin or destination of the trip.

The driver is next questioned about the purposes of his journey and what he was doing before starting the trip (e.g. going home from work; going shopping from home). A typical transportation study in a conurbation would subdivide the journey purposes into as many as eleven classes. However, for a small or medium-sized town fewer classes of journey purpose are usually defined. Basically these are similar to the journey purposes distinguished in the home-interview study.

In certain cases additional questions concerning a possible intermediate stop within the area under study and the reasons for it are asked of people making through trips.

Whilst the interviewers at the survey point are questioning the sample selected for interview, a continuous record of all vehicles passing through the point is kept by enumerators. This count is a classified vehicle count, and is usually recorded on the standard Ministry of Transport Enumerators Form, although in certain cases tally counters are used.

Both interviews and the total vehicle enumeration are carried out for a set time interval—usually fifteen or thirty minutes. As soon as this chosen period of time elapses a fresh count for the next time period is commenced, regardless of the number of entries recorded.

Each cordon station is usually in operation for sixteen hours daily, from 6 a.m. to 10 p.m., and is operated by staff working in two shifts. The numbers required to operate the station depends on the traffic volume, the number of questions asked, and the size of sample selected. As a rule of thumb it is estimated that one interviewer should be able to cope with approximately eighty vehicles per hour.[9] It is standard practice to have a police constable on duty to direct traffic and select the vehicles for interview on the instructions of the site supervisor. The size of sample interviewed varies with the accuracy required in grossing up, and the volume of traffic on a particular route.

Sample selection at cordon surveys

Three main types of sampling procedure can be employed on a cordon survey.

1 *Time cluster sampling*—when during each hour or time interval of the survey a period of time is selected when all vehicle drivers are interviewed, and a further period of time when no interviews are carried out. This method allows the interviewers to alternate interview directions to cover both inward and outward movements.

2 *Volume cluster sampling*—the number of vehicles to be interviewed is predetermined, depending on the sample size adopted. Similarly a predetermined number of vehicles is allowed to pass without interviewing.

3 *Variable rate sampling*—This method of random sampling was developed by the Road Research Laboratory and is the method normally used at cordon surveys.[10] Interviewers are employed at a constant rate, and the size of sample selected varies with the volume of traffic flow. Depending on the characteristics of the stream, sample rates are calculated for either half-hour or one-hour periods. To reduce bias different sample rates are usually calculated for different classes of vehicle.

Public transport trips

Public transport trips by bus or rail which originate outside the external cordon, but have a destination within it, may form a small proportion of the total travel in the area under study. However, they are usually of sufficient importance to warrant the collection of full information about them.

A variety of techniques can be adopted to assemble this information. Because of the problems associated with interviewing on a crowded bus or train the most favoured method is the pre-paid business reply postcard. This is issued to passengers as they board either bus or train and they are requested to complete the questionnaire and return the postcard to the survey headquarters. The survey of rail passengers undertaken as part of the *London Traffic Survey* adopted a variation on this theme by asking rail passengers to complete the questionnaire whilst travelling into the central London termini, and hand it in at a 'collection point' on arrival. However, problems associated with the low returns, and a biased sample still remain, although in an attempt to overcome this more recent transportation studies use the pre-paid postcards as lottery tickets so that for each card correctly completed and returned the person interviewed stands a chance of winning a prize.

Another technique adopted with some success, especially in West Germany, is to use an interviewer with a tape recorder to collect information about public transport trips across the external cordon. This method allows a large sample to be interviewed, and coding to be undertaken the same evening.

In areas where the volume of bus passenger traffic across the external cordon is light it is possible to use an interviewer, boarding the bus, noting the number of people on the bus and interviewing a sample of those present.

The information required from both bus and rail passengers is similar to that required at the roadside interview—namely place of origin and destination, purpose of journey, and (depending on the purpose of the study) mode of travel adopted prior to boarding bus or train, and mode of travel to be adopted on leaving the bus or train.

Internal cordon or screen line counts

Volumetric counts of traffic crossing an internal cordon or screen line are made, to compare the estimated number of trips derived from grossed-up interview returns, with the trips actually observed on the road. These counts can be carried out automatically, or manually.

If only one screen line is chosen it should divide the study area into approximately two equal halves, but should not pass through the central area. To minimise the number of survey points on the screen line it is best to utilise a barrier to movement such as a river or a railway.

In exceptional circumstances the procedures used at the external cordon are also adopted on the screen line or internal cordon. However, because of the congestion and delays to traffic and the additional expense involved, this happens only rarely.

Commercial vehicle survey

To obtain full information about commercial vehicle trips taking place within the external cordon it is necessary to take a sample of all the commercial vehicles garaged within the area, and interview the owner or driver responsible for the vehicles chosen. No definite guidance is available about the size of sample to be selected, but it is generally accepted that for a small town a sample approaching 100% could well be necessary, whereas in a larger area a sample of less than 30% would be considered satisfactory.

The sample frame from which the vehicles are selected is usually the record of vehicle excise licences for the area under consideration. This should relate to the same period of time as the household interview sample. There are several problems associated with using this sample frame. Vehicles registered in the study area but used continuously elsewhere present a problem which is especially associated with fleet operators: vehicles recently transferred to new owners outside the study area, or recently scrapped or out of service for repair can upset the sample frame.

The vehicle owner or operator might refuse to supply the information requested, or the vehicle selected for interview might not have been used on the day for which travel data is required. These problems can only be determined at the time of interview, when the appropriate course of action is to record the situation on the interview forms, so that appropriate adjustments can be made for these vehicles when the expansion factor is calculated.

Figure 6 shows a typical Commercial Vehicle Survey Form; the information normally collected consists of (1) *Vehicle information*—including the registration number of the vehicle, name and address of the firm or owners (these are usually entered in the office before the interview is undertaken), and the name and address of the depot from which the vehicle operated on the survey date and the vehicle type.

Fig. 6 (Overleaf) Typical commercial vehicle interview form

WYCOMBE AREA TRANSPORTATION STUDY

COMMERCIAL VEHICLE SURVEY

Zone........ Code No......... Page.......of.........

VEHICLE INFORMATION

			ADMINISTRATIVE RECORD				
			INTERVIEWER				

	Card type	1	LETTER SENT			TEL.	
Registration No.	Traffic zone	2		CALLS	DATE	TIME	RESULT
	Code No.	5					
SURVEY DAY	SURVEY DATE	Expansion factor	8				
		Seasonal factor	11				

NAME & ADDRESS OF FIRM (OR OWNER) | 14

INTERVIEW COMPLETED	INTERVIEW NOT COMPLETED
COMMENTS	
FIELD CHECK	OFFICE CHECK
CODING COMPLETED	CODING CHECKED

VEHICLE TYPE (Tick appropriate box)
- [ ] Car with 'C' licence
- [ ] Light goods (under 30 cwt. unladen)
- [ ] Heavy goods (over 30 cwt. unladen)
- [ ] Private coach or bus
- [ ] Taxi

ADDRESS OF DEPOT (FROM WHICH VEHICLE OPERATED ON SURVEY DAY)

JOURNEY INFORMATION

Journey No.	ORIGIN Precise address if in Study Area	DESTINATION Precise address if in Study Area	TIME Start	TIME Finish	JOURNEY PURPOSE Tick appropriate box	Number of PASSENGERS including driver	TRIP TYPE
	15	18	A.M. / P.M. 21	A.M. / P.M.	□ Firm's business □ To or from home □ Personal business 23	24	26
	28	31	A.M. / P.M. 34	A.M. / P.M.	□ Firm's business □ To or from home □ Personal business 36	37	39
			A.M. / P.M.	A.M. / P.M.	□ Firm's business □ To or from home		

Firm's business
To or from home
Personal business

A.M.
P.M.

54	57	60	62	63	65		
15	18	21	23	24	26		
28	31	34	36	37	39		
41	44	47	49	50	52		
54	57	60	62	63	65		

To or from home
Personal business

Firm's business
To or from home
Personal business   A.M.   P.M.

15	18	21	23	24	26
28	31	34	36	37	39
41	44	47	49	50	52
54	57	60	62	63	65

Study Area:

High Wycombe
Beamond End
Bolter End
Booker
Bradenham

Bryant's Bottom
Cryers Hill
Downley
Fingest
Flackwell Heath

Great Kingshill
Hazlemere
Heath End
Holmer Green
Hughenden

Lane End
Loudwater
Lower North Dean
Naphill
Penn

Piddington
Terriers
Tylers Green
Upper North Dean
Walter's Ash

West Wycombe
Widmer End
Wooburn Green

2 *Journey information*—this relates to one way travel between two essential stops. It does not include stops for traffic jams, accidents and other delays. Journeys should be numbered consecutively for each vehicle, beginning with No. 1 for the first trip, No. 2 for the second and so on, and information about the origin and destination and the time taken for each trip must be collected. As with the external cordon count exact addresses for origins and destinations within the study area must be given. In the larger transportation studies as many as ten commercial journey purposes may be defined, although it is usual to consider only three main purposes:

   a Firm's business

   b To or from home

   c Personal business

Difficulty may sometimes be encountered in obtaining exact information about the movements of a particular vehicle on the survey day, especially when the vehicle has made a number of different journeys. To overcome this problem log-books are sometimes issued to the drivers of the appropriate vehicles at the start of the survey day, so that the correct journey information can be entered as each journey is completed.[11]

Taxi survey

In large towns or cities where taxis are an important element in the public transport system, a separate survey of taxi movements is usually carried out. The procedure adopted is identical to that used in the Commercial Vehicle Survey, although owing to the comparatively limited size of the sample population the sample size adopted tends to be larger.

Survey of existing transport facilities

An important element of the collection of basic data is the survey of existing transport facilities. It is, in effect, a stock-taking of the major highway and public transport networks, the existing demand for and supply of parking accommodation, and the present-day traffic volumes and travel times.

This data is required for use in the trip distribution and assignment stage of the transportation planning process.

1 *Main road inventory*

The limited capacity of the computer, and the amount of work involved, normally results in the survey of the physical characteristics of the road network being restricted to the main or primary network. The designation of this primary network is based on the volume and nature of traffic carried, the existing road classification, and the requirements of the traffic assignment procedures to be adopted.

Following the designation of a primary network, its basic characteristics in terms of local, regional and national functions are determined. Within the survey area the nature, extent and density of development adjacent to, and fronting on, the network are examined. Particularly important are the number and frequency of frontage accesses. Carriageway widths, traffic regulations, visibility conditions, junction spacing and capacities, especially at critical points, are also important. Analysis of this survey data will highlight those parts of the road network operating at less than capacity. In addition the number, location and extent of any bottlenecks on the network will also be revealed.

2 *Public transport inventory*

The designation of public transport networks is slightly more complicated than the designation of road networks. In the large urban areas both rail and bus facilities will be available for internal movements, but for the smaller built up areas only bus transport will be of interest.

The identification of the railway network is a comparatively straightforward matter, which can be done from a route map and timetable. The capacity of the various services can only be obtained by field studies, or with the co-operation of British Rail. It is usual for the public transport operators to participate in the transportation planning process, and in addition to current passenger volumes carried, they also provide details about fare structure and future proposals.[12]

A similar procedure is adopted in identifying a bus network. Principal routes, stopping places, and travel times can be derived from route maps and the operator's time-table. However, buses are invariably delayed by traffic congestion, especially during the peak periods, and to obtain the actual rather than the scheduled running time of the services, a check is made in the field. In addition, links must be added into the public transport network to represent time spent walking and waiting at the terminal and interchange points.

3 Traffic volume census

Traffic volume counts are made at the external cordon, the internal cordon if operated, the internal screen lines, and any other position considered necessary. The purpose of the counts is to establish typical patterns of hourly, daily and seasonal variations in the traffic flow. These counts can be made manually, using the standard Ministry of Transport Enumeration Form, or banked tally counters, but the more normal practice is to use automatic recording counters in conjunction with sample manual classified counts to determine the composition of the traffic flow.[13] Pedestrian counts of movements across the carriageway are sometimes undertaken at conflict points.[14]

4 Travel-time Survey

Travel times, and speed-flow relationships for both peak and off-peak periods are used as a basis for determining the present level of service performed by the system, and in the distribution and assignment stages of the transportation planning process. The 'moving-observer method', devised by the Road Research Laboratory, is considered to be the most efficient and reliable way of collecting this information for motor vehicles.[15] Basically the procedure involves an observer

1 making a trip in a motor vehicle over a specified length of

the road network, both with and against the traffic stream he is surveying.

2 counting the number of oncoming vehicles when travelling against the stream of traffic being surveyed.

3 counting the number of vehicles overtaking the test car, and the number of moving vehicles overtaken by the test car

4 measuring the times taken for the journey with, and against, the stream being surveyed.

From the formulae

q =flow vehicles per minute

$\bar{t}$ =mean journey time

x =vehicles met when travelling against the stream

y =vehicles overtaking test car minus vehicles overtaken by test car

ta =time against stream

tw =time with stream

(i) $q = \dfrac{(x+y)}{(ta+tw)}$ (Flow)

(ii) $\bar{t} = tw - \dfrac{y}{q}$ (Mean journey time)

the flow of vehicles in the stream (in vehicles per minute) and the mean journey time can be calculated.

The run over each leg is repeated for a minimum of six times and x, y, ta, and tw are replaced by the average values for the total number of runs.

Mean journey times can be obtained for different classes of vehicle if x and y are counted for the different classes of vehicle.

5 *Parking survey*

'It appears absolutely essential that the public authority should retain complete control of

1 the amount of parking space that is provided

2 its location, and

3 the charges that are levied.

and it should be prepared to use this control methodically as part of the transportation plan.'[16]

As part of the transportation planning process parking

63

investigations are undertaken to collect information about the physical location, type, capacity, layout and operating characteristics of existing on- and off-street parking facilities within the central area.[17] The number of legal parking spaces is determined by a field survey—as are other factors such as specially reserved spaces for lorry loading, bus stops, taxi stands, hotel entrances, and areas within the vicinity of junctions, pedestrian walks, and driveways where parking is prohibited. Time limits and other restrictions of the use of legal metered and non-metered parking spaces are determined. The rates charged for metered on-street spaces and off-street facilities are recorded. This data is then processed to determine the total parking supply in the central area.

The existing parking demand within the central area is determined by means of a count of parkers within the district. The method usually adopted is to record the licence plate of each legally and illegally parked vehicle at intervals of time not exceeding thirty minutes, between the hours of 7 a.m.–7 p.m. on a weekday. This data when analysed will indicate the occupancy and turnover of parking spaces within the area.

In addition parking information collected in the field is used in conjunction with the information collected in the home-interview study, on destination, type of parking and distance walked after parking, to determine the existing parking demand.

Planning and economic data

The *Traffic in Towns Report* quite clearly demonstrated that the movement of goods and people by either public transport or private motor vehicle is inextricably linked with the distribution and intensity of land use.

'Vehicles do not of course move about the roads for mysterious reasons of their own. They move only because people want them to move in connection with activities which they (the people) are engaged in. Traffic is therefore a function of activities ... and traffic is concentrated in town because activities are concentrated there. It is characteristic of activities in towns that they mainly take place in buildings or

64

in places such as markets, depots, docks and stations. . . . In towns therefore traffic can be said to be the function of buildings.'[18]

It is this relationship which forms the basis of transportation planning, whereby present-day trip generation rates are established for different land-use, population and economic characteristics. These planning factors are then predicted for the target date, and future trip generation rates estimated using the predicted planning data, and the present-day relationship between trip generation and planning data.

1 *Population and employment data*

The type of planning data collected varies with the size, purpose and organisation of the study being carried out. However, certain elements are fundamental to all studies. For each internal traffic zone, basic population statistics are essential. Experience has shown that the total zonal population is a significant factor in estimating trip generation. In addition some indication of the age/sex, and household structure of the zonal population is required. In some instances this can take the form of a simple indication of the number of persons of five years of age and above. In other cases the age structure can be given in considerable detail covering the groups 0–4 yr, 5–14 yr, 15–24 yr, 25–44 yr, 45–59 yr, and 60 and over, although a fewer number categories would probably be more satisfactory. The household structure of a zone can similarly be given in an unsophisticated way such as the total number of households, or can be subdivided into categories based on different household sizes.

Information relating to the size and structure of the labour force is also required for each internal zone. This data can be simply the crude total of residents who are in employment, or it can be presented in more detail by breaking it down into significant groupings by age and sex.

The most comprehensive source for this data is the Census of Population which provides all the above information for Enumeration Districts, parishes and wards throughout the country. However, there are two basic problems associated with using the census as a source of population data.

1 Enumeration Districts are arbitrarily defined areas, based broadly on the amount of information it is possible for a census enumerator to collect in one day. They rarely coincide with traffic zone boundaries. Consequently, difficulty is experienced in providing reliable population statistics for each traffic zone.

2 Until the 1966 10% Sample Census, the Census of Population was carried out dicennially, with the result that any data used was often several years out of date.

Consequently, the Census of Population tends to be used in transportation studies largely as a check against population data collected in the home-interview study, rather than as a basic source of data. However, the introduction of a 10% Sample Census, to take place every ten years, between the full censuses (which will continue to be carried out dicenially) will eliminate to a certain extent, the disadvantages associated with the Census being out of date when used.

The incompatibility of Enumeration Districts and traffic zones could be overcome if the census information were to be collected for areas related to National Grid References and in the 1971 Census, the Registrar General will present, as an experiment and for a limited area only, census data relating to 100 metre squares. Should this prove to be a success and the method adopted generally for later census, then the question of incompatibility of Enumeration Districts and traffic zones will be largely eliminated. Other less radical attempts have been made in recent years to overcome this problem and perhaps the most successful method has been that adopted by Essex County Council. In several studies they have conducted, Enumeration Districts have been used as traffic zones. In those instances where traffic zone requirements have been in conflict with the Enumeration District, then planning data, and movements have been coded to both the Enumeration District and a super-imposed traffic zone.

For all internal zones employment data is required which relates to the total number of jobs, and the break-down of these jobs into the type of employment. This grouping of

66

employment data should be based on the Standard Industrial Classification, although the number of classes used can vary with the purpose and scope of the study.[19] It is usual to identify at least three types of employment category distinguishing between extractive/primary, manufacturing, and service employment. In the larger transportation studies the types of employment are often classified into as many as nine groups covering manufacturing industry, non-manufacturing industry, retail trade, personal services, business and professional, wholesale trade and storage, public service, recreation and other.

The Ministry of Labour Employment Register, which is compiled annually, provides a record for each Employment Exchange Area of the total number of people employed in each firm or establishment employing five persons or more. It is not published but access to the information can be obtained through the regional officers of the Ministry of Labour. There are several problems associated with using this Register as a basic source of employment data:

1 the data relates only to firm's employing five persons or more. It is therefore not a complete coverage, nor can it be regarded as a random sample

2 the data relates to Employment Exchange Areas, which are invariably unrelated to traffic zones

3 frequently the latest Register is several years out of date

4 establishments with branch offices may have all their employees registered at the head office, despite the fact that they may be dispersed throughout the country.

As a result of these problems the Ministry of Labour Register is only rarely used as a source of employment data in transportation studies. It is usual practice to carry out a special survey to derive the required information.

This survey can be a sample survey or a complete coverage, and the sample frame is usually derived from the Valuation Rolls. Special investigations are also initiated to determine employment premises not listed in the rolls. Information from the home-interview study relating to destinations for employment are used as a check against the employment survey data.

67

The introduction of journey to work questions into the 1966 Sample Census, and the availability of this data at Enumeration District level provides another source of employment data, in a form which could be used in the transportation planning process. Detailed information is provided concerning the destination of all those in employment, the industry of employment by Standard Industrial Classification, and the mode of travel to work. However, the problem of the probable incompatibility of Enumeration Districts and traffic zones remains.

2 *Income*

The level of income in a household affects the number, frequency and mode of trips made by the residents. Consequently, as part of the transportation planning process, data is required about the income levels in each traffic zone. One method of obtaining this information is by asking a direct question about household income as part of the home-interview study. However, the population at large is generally reluctant to answer such personal questions and if answers are given there is a strong possibility that they will be incorrect anyway.

An indication of levels of income in each zone is therefore derived indirectly from an analysis of those factors which reflect income and for which information is more readily available. Levels of car ownership—derived from the Excise licence records kept by the Local Authorities—the proportion of owner-occupied dwellings in the zone, or alternatively the proportion of council-rented properties—derived from Valuation Rolls, or Local Authority records—the socio-economic group of the chief economic supporter—derived from an analysis of occupation by socio-economic group—are all popular and generally adopted indicators.

The 1966 10% Sample Census provides the bulk of this information, at Enumeration District level, giving details of

1 the total number of cars owned, the number of households with nil, one and two or more cars

2 the number of owner-occupied dwellings, council-rented

dwellings, other rented dwellings furnished and unfurnished, and 'other' dwellings

3 the socio-economic group of the chief economic supporter of the household

4 the social class of the chief economic supporter of the household. However, the problem of incompatibility of Enumeration Districts and traffic zones still remains to be overcome.

3 *Retail sales*

The number of trips made to the central area for shopping purposes is reflected in the volume of retail sales, and/or the retail floor area. Data relating to these two factors is therefore required in the transportation planning process; in some instances all that is required are the crude totals for all shopping centres within the survey area. In the more sophisticated studies, the volume of retail sales is classified into sales of day-to-day goods, and durable goods; and the retail floor area into 'selling' space and storage space. Floor-space data can be derived either from a land-use survey, or an examination of the Valuation Rolls. Statistics concerning sales for the various retail and service trades are obtainable from official publications for towns with a population of 25,000 and over.[20] A more detailed breakdown of this same information for smaller towns, and for different shopping centres within the same town or conurbation is available on request from the Board of Trade. Although these statistics have the disadvantage of

1 relating only to the returns received by the Board of Trade, and

2 being subject to 'confidentiality' thereby precluding the disclosure of much information for small centres

they are nevertheless the most reliable available source of this data.

4 *Attendance at schools, colleges and other educational establishments*

Information about the location, and number of attendances at Primary and Secondary schools and Further Educational establishments is required for each internal zone. This data is obtained from Local Authority records. If necessary the home-interview study results can be used as a check.

5 Other land-use data

It has been found that both the amount and the characteristics of travel are influenced by the intensity of development of land. For residential areas—the areas from which the bulk of travel is generated—this intensity of use is measured in terms of residential density. Net residential density is the measure most typically used and is defined as the ratio of the resident population or the number of dwellings or the number of habitable rooms to the acreage of all land used for residential purposes, plus half the width of the surrounding roads up to a maximum of twenty feet.

For employment zones and the central area—the areas to which most trips are attracted—the intensity of use is measured in terms of Plot Ratio or Floor Space Index. The former is defined as the ratio of usable floor space to the net site area. The latter is defined as the ratio of total floor space to the site area plus half the width of roads up to a maximum of twenty feet.

Evaluation of survey accuracy

It is desirable to check the accuracy of the survey data before the process of analysis is completely under way. This is done by comparing it with facts that are either already known, or obtained as part of the survey process.

1 Home interview—dwelling-unit sample

The accuracy of the dwelling-unit sample selection can be estimated by comparing the population of each Enumeration District or traffic zone, as determined from the expanded home-interview data, with the population derived from census data. The census data, however, must be adjusted to take account of changes which may have occurred since that information was compiled.

70

To avoid unnecessary expense a preliminary check should be done manually before the tabulating cards are punched. If at all possible it should be carried out as the interviewing is completed in each zone or area, so that if the comparison is not satisfactory the source of the trouble can be determined immediately and steps taken to rectify the situation before the work is too advanced.

Expanded home-interview data should not vary by more than ± 15% of the adjusted census data. If an unsatisfactory comparison does result then the two possible causes are

1 an inadequate or poorly selected sample
2 unsatisfactory work on the part of the interviewers.

The cause can be determined by carrying out spot checks at sample dwellings previously interviewed, and if this shows the interviewers to be at fault then they should either be given further instruction on interviewing procedure or they should be replaced by other trained interviewers. If necessary, parts or all of the zones showing unsatisfactory comparisons should be re-interviewed.

If the spot checks indicate that an inadequate or poorly chosen sample is the cause of poor comparisons, then the procedure of sample selection should be re-examined and if necessary a modified sample chosen.

2 *Accuracy of travel-pattern data*

The accuracy of travel-pattern data recorded in the home-interview study and the roadside interviews, can be checked in a variety of ways each of which involves preparatory work before the survey commences. Perhaps the most satisfactory method of checking motor vehicle trip data is the use of a screen line. The object of a screen line is to divide the area bounded by the external cordon into two, and to compare the actual traffic flows across the line with those reported in the home-interview study. The screen line chosen should preferably be a natural barrier, such as a river or railway, with comparatively few crossing points. It should be straight to avoid vehicles crossing it more than once on the same trip; it should not pass through the central area where the complexity of vehicle trips is almost certain to involve vehicles crossing and recrossing it on the same trip; and it should not pass too close to the external cordon. An alternative to the use of a screen line is the use of two or three control points, preferably in different parts of the study area. Viaducts, bridges, underpasses or other well-known points through which large volumes of traffic pass, are most suitable locations for these control points, and the objective is to compare the actual vehicle trips passing through the control point with the number of trips reported in the home and road-side interviews which should pass through the same control point.

The traffic counts carried out at both the screen line and the control points are similar, and include the use of automatic vehicle counters, recording total traffic flows in one hourly periods, supplemented by classified manual counts.

In addition to the checks provided by the screen line or control points, data collected at the external cordon roadside interviews can be used to assess the accuracy of the trips across the external cordon reported in the home-interview study by residents and commercial vehicle operators within the external cordon.

A comparison of the reported public transport trips with the total public transport movements for an average day, derived from the public transport operators, will reveal any discrepancies in this particular field.

The accuracy with which journeys to and from work have been reported can be assessed by comparing the number of persons employed in a particular zone, with the work trips into the zone as derived from the expanded-interview data. Allowance must be made for absenteeism and persons walking to work.

Analysis

1 *Coding and punching*

Before the data collected by the interviewers can be processed it must be coded into a predetermined series of number forms.

This coded information is then punched on to paper tape or punched cards for mechanical sorting and processing. Occasionally the interview forms used in the field are so arranged that the results are entered on the form in the appropriate code, as the interview takes place. This process, however, places additional strain on the interviewer, and in practice it has been found that it is safer to use special staff to code the data in the office.

The coding operation is repetitive and tedious, and in an attempt to eliminate confusion and errors the process is usually broken down into a series of operations, each performed by an individual member of the coding staff, e.g. one person codes the origins and destinations only, another codes mode of travel and so on. Once the data has been coded it is transferred to punched cards or paper tape by specially trained operators, and is used in this form as the computer input.

2 Expansion factors

Data collected at the different types of field survey, which utilise a sampling procedure, must be expanded to represent the whole population, and to account for missed interviews. This is achieved through the use of expansion factors and ordinarily they are calculated for each zone used in the survey:
1 The expansion factor used for the home-interview study is basically the total universe, i.e. the total number of households in the survey area divided by the total number of successful interviews. This is calculated from the following formula, for each traffic zone.

$$\text{Expansion Factor} = \frac{A - \dfrac{A}{B}(C + \dfrac{C}{B} \times D)}{B - C - D}$$

where A = total number of addresses on original list
B = total number of addresses selected as original sample
C = number of sample addresses that are ineligible (e.g. demolished, non-residential)
D = number of sample addresses where no response is made (e.g. refusal to answer, no reply)

2 The external cordon survey expansion factor is usually derived for each class of vehicle, time interval and direction of flow used at the survey point. It is calculated from the following formula.

$$\text{Expansion Factor} = \frac{A}{B}$$

where A=the number of vehicles of the specified class counted passing through the survey point for the relevant time interval.

B=the number of vehicles interviewed, of the same class and for the same time interval.

In addition '24-hour' factors are required to bring to a 24-hour basis the information collected at the external cordon stations operated for a 16-hour period only. This is achieved from the following formula.

$$\text{24-hour expansion factor} = R \times \frac{A}{B}$$

R=Average expansion factor for time interval

A=Average count for 'n' days for vehicles of appropriate class passing through survey point in 24 hours

B=Average count for 'n' days for vehicles of appropriate class passing through survey point during the period of time interviews are made

3 The Commercial Vehicle Survey expansion factor is derived in the same way as the home-interview survey expansion factor; from the formula

$$\text{Expansion Factor} = \frac{A - \frac{A}{B}(C + \frac{C}{B} \times D)}{B - C - D}$$

where A=total number of registrations on the original list

B=number of registrations chosen as the sample

C=number of vehicles in the sample disposed of or unlicensed

D=number of vehicles for which refusals are recorded

A separate factor is usually calculated for each traffic zone.

3 'Through' trips

In theory 'through' trips will cross the external cordon twice, and will therefore be interviewed twice. The standard method of eliminating this duplication is to punch a o·5 expansion factor in all 'through' trip records. Alternatively the processed tabulated values for through trips can be divided by two.

4 Tabulations

Data collected in the various stages of a transportation study is comprehensive, and can be presented in many different forms. With the advantage of hindsight it is frequently possible to say '... too many tabulations were certainly prepared, and some have never been used'.[21] To eliminate, as far as possible, the danger of such a situation arising, it is usual to prepare, in the initial stages, standard tabulations required for all transportation studies. At the same time care should be taken to ensure that the coded data in its punched state, or converted to magnetic tape, is so arranged as to facilitate the processing of any tabulations that may later be required.

Conclusions

The collection of this basic data relating to the existing situation poses many problems, but these are insignificant when compared with the problems associated with the projection of this same data to the target date. In the last half-century change has been occurring at a tremendous rate. Changes in the technological, and demographic spheres ensure that it is impossible to predict accurately population trends for more than 5–10 years ahead, whilst economic advances have led to changes in the pattern of industrial growth, and the requirements and standards demanded by the population generally. In an attempt to estimate the future course of events numerous assumptions have to be made in the transportation planning process, with the result than any conclusions derived must be treated with caution.

References

1 Fisher R. J. and Sosslau A. B., Census data as a Source for urban transportation planning, *Highway Research Board Record No. 141*, (1966).
2 Sheath R. and Lee N. H., Zoning by National Grid References, *Traffic Engineering and Control* (1965).
3 Ministry of Transport, *Standard Classifications for Traffic and Transport*, H.M.S.O. London (1964).
4 Taylor M. A., *Zoning for Urban Travel Studies*, Road Research Laboratory LN/415/MAT (1963) (unpublished).
5 Sheath R. and Lee N. H., *op. cit.*
6 Conducting a home-interview origin and destination survey, *Procedure Manual—National Committee on Urban Transportation*, Public Administration Service, Chicago (1954).
7 *Memorandum on Land Use/Transport Studies for Medium Sized Towns*, Ministry of Transport (1966) (unpublished).
8 Buchanan Colin and Partners, *Bath: A Planning and Transport Study* (1965).
9 Ministry of Transport, Scottish Development Department, *Urban Traffic Engineering Techniques*, H.M.S.O. London (1965).
10 Road Research Laboratory, *Research on Road Traffic,* Traffic Surveys (chapter 4), H.M.S.O. London (1965).
11 Anderson J. E. F., Transportation studies: a review of results to date from typical areas—Belfast. *Proceedings of the Transportation Engineering Conference* organised by the Institution of Civil Engineers, London (1968).
12 For example: The co-operation of British Rail, the Scottish Bus Group, and the Glasgow Corporation Transport Department in the *Greater Glasgow Transportation Study* has facilitated the collection of data concerning fare structure, current passenger volumes, operating schedules and planned new routes.
13 See *Measuring Traffic Volumes—Procedure Manual*, National

Committee on Urban Transportation, Public Administration
Service, Chicago (1958).

14 See *Urban Traffic Engineering Techniques*, Para. 55–59, *op. cit.*

15 Wardrop J. B. and Charlesworth G., A method of estimating
speed and flow of traffic from a moving vehicle. *Proceedings
of the Institution of Civil Engineers*, Part II, Volume 3 (1954).

16 Buchanan C. D., *Traffic in Towns—Reports of the Steering Group
and Working Group*, Para. 452, H.M.S.O. London (1963).

17 See (i) *Parking*, Eno Foundation, Saugatauk, Connecticut
(1957).
(ii) *Parking in Town Centres*, Ministry of Housing and Local
Government, and the Ministry of Transport, H.M.S.O. (1965).

18 Buchanan C. D., *Traffic in Towns, op. cit.*

19 See Central Statistical Office, *Standard Industrial Classification*,
H.M.S.O. London (1959).

20 See Board of Trade, *Census of Distribution 1961*, H.M.S.O.
London (1961).

21 Martin B. V., Transportation studies: a review of results
from typical areas—1. London. *Proceedings of the Transportation
Engineering Conference* organised by the Institution of Civil
Engineers, London (1968).

SOURCE (For Figs. 4–6) Wycombe Area Transportation Study—
Interview Manual, County Surveyor, County Planning Officer,
Buckinghamshire County Council, Borough Engineer and Surveyor,
High Wycombe.

3 Trip generation

Introduction

The trip generation stage of the transportation planning process is concerned with the prediction of future levels of person or vehicular travel, usually for traffic zones or combinations of traffic zones known as traffic districts. The techniques developed attempt to utilise the observed relationships between travel characteristics and the urban environment, and are based on the assumption that 'trip making is a function of three basic factors:

1 The land-use pattern and developments in the study area.
2 The socio-economic characteristics of the trip-making population of the study area.
3 The nature, extent and capabilities of the transportation system in the study area.'[1]

These basic factors can be represented by a variety of inter-dependent variables whose influence changes both with the geographic location of the study area, and with different time periods. Trip generation studies are a vital part of the trans-portation planning process—it is essential that the present-day determinants of trip production be understood before the nature of the future travel demand can be assessed. Once the significant land-use, population and transport characteristics influencing travel demand have been identified, they are projected to the target date to provide estimates of the total amount and kind of travel demand.

As part of the trip generation study it is normal practice to estimate the number of trips originating in each traffic zone, i.e. trip productions, and the number of trips destined for each zone, i.e. trip attractions. This is to ensure that at the distribution stage of the process different combinations of trips which are not necessarily reversible can be adequately catered for, e.g. a typical combination of trips made by one person throughout the day might be from home to work; from work to recreation (cinema) and from recreation to home. In this case the trip production is from home to work, whilst the attraction to home is from recreation. Indeed, the more commonly used synthetic distribution models incorporate both trip productions and trip attractions in their basic framework.

Depending on the design of the overall study process, trip generation models can be derived for person or vehicular movements, by trip purpose and time of day, e.g. if the study is designed to incorporate a trip end modal split model (i.e. the allocation of the various movements to different modes of transport before the generated trips are distributed between the traffic zones), then the trip generation model could be designed to derive trip productions in terms of person movements by different modes of travel. If on the other hand a trip interchange modal split model is to be used, which allocates different portions of the total trip movements between zones to the various travel modes after the trip distribution stage, then the trip generation model could be designed to derive trip productions in terms of total person movements. Similarly, since person trips having different trip purposes present different trip distribution and modal split characteristics, it is often considered essential to stratify trips by purpose throughout the transportation planning process. This in turn implies that trip generation analysis must be undertaken for different trip purposes. The number of different trip purposes used varies with the design of the individual study. A typical stratification of home-based trips could well take the following form:

1 From home to work
2 From home to shop

3 From home to other
4 From work to home
5 From shop to home
6 From other to home

The generation of non-home-based trips, e.g. delivery of goods from one industrial plant to another is usually estimated in terms of vehicle movements. Depending on the design of the study this can be stratified into the different types of vehicle making these non-home-based movements, or can be estimated as total vehicle movements produced or attracted. A typical stratification could be into light, medium and heavy commercial vehicles.

Factors influencing trip generation

1 Land-use factors

Land use is a convenient way of classifying trip generating activities, because it is a factor which in Britain can be predicted with a reasonable degree of accuracy, and is readily measured. Different uses of land produce different trip generation characteristics, e.g. land given over to shopping development or offices could be expected to generate more trips than open space.

Similarly the intensity with which different activities are pursued can produce different generation characteristics, e.g. one acre of residential land developed at a high density would be likely to produce more total person movements than one acre of land developed for residential purposes at a low density. On the other hand, the low-density residential area occupied by fewer and probably more expensive dwellings could well produce more private motor vehicle trips than the high-density residential area.

Although the range of urban land uses is extensive, for the purposes of trip generation studies it is usual to consider only the most significant uses. Since between 80–90% of all journeys have either a beginning or an end in the home, residential land use is of prime importance. The measure of residential development used in trip generation studies varies with the type of study being undertaken. It can for example be represented in terms of acres of residential land, number of dwelling units, number of dwelling units per acre, number of persons per acre, or total population.

Commercial and industrial land use, as employment centres are the next most significant land uses in connection with trip generation, and as different types of commercial and industrial activities produce different generation rates it is usual to distinguish between manufacturing and service industry, retail and wholesale distribution, and office employment. A variety of measures of intensity of these activities can be used, but the most common tend to be the numbers employed per unit area of land; and the land area given over to, or the amount of floor space occupied by, such activities.

Other uses of land considered to be significant in terms of trip generation are educational and recreational developments. Educational establishments such as universities, technical colleges and comprehensive schools are large generators of movement and in many cases warrant particular attention, e.g. the *Guildford Study*, carried out by Buchanan and Partners included a comprehensive study of the effect of the development of the University of Surrey on trip generation and distribution in Guildford.[2]

The most commonly used measure of the intensity of development at an educational institution tends to be the numbers in attendance. Small recreational facilities can by and large be ignored in the transportation planning process, but there are exceptional cases where careful consideration must be paid to these uses, e.g. large regional parks such as the proposed Lea Valley Regional Park and the Central London area of concentrated theatre and entertainment developments.

2 *The Home*[3]

1 *Family size:* Travel is a function of human activity. Consequently a relationship should exist between the number and frequency of trips made from the home and family size. Schuldiner in his work on the Modesto area of California has

shown that average trip frequency increases with increasing persons per household, at the rate of approximately 0·8 trips per day for each additional person. This increase in the number of trips with family size is, however, related mainly to non-work trips which tend to level off at the four person per dwelling unit family size.

2 *Motor vehicle ownership:* The ability to satisfy travel demands is affected by the availability of alternative means of transport and the adequacy of the highway system. Motor vehicle ownership, or the number of vehicles available for use by each household, has been found to have a significant influence on trip generation. Households with more than one motor vehicle tend to generate more trips per unit than households with only one motor vehicle, although the single car households tend to utilise their vehicle more intensively.

Motor vehicle ownership and family size are to a certain extent related. Generally speaking it is the larger family which has the higher level of car ownership. It would appear that the greater trip generation inherent in larger families is only fully realised where sufficient motor vehicles are available for use by members of the family. Thus a large non-motor-vehicle-owning family can be expected to generate fewer trips than the same size family which has access to three motor vehicles. A variety of measures of car ownership can be used, the most common of which are the total number of cars per zone, car ownership per person, or car ownership per household.

3 *Type of dwelling unit:* It can be argued that the more permanent types of dwelling unit such as a single family house, reflect a high degree of integration into the local community on the part of the household, and leads to a high rate of trip generation. Conversely the less permanent dwellings, e.g. an hotel room, result in a more limited integration with local affairs, with a lower resultant trip generation rate. Indeed Schuldiner found that this was the case although the difference was not as marked as was expected, e.g. although the average number of 'from home' trips increased with the permanency of the dwelling type, when family size and car-ownership levels were taken into consideration, the difference in generation rates was not as great as appeared at first sight.

4 *Occupied residents:* The occupation of the head of the household is one of the major indicators of the standard of living enjoyed by the family and reflects to a certain extent the family income. In general terms it has been found that the proportion of work trips for the gainfully employed groups decreases as the occupational status increases, although the proportion of trips for non-work purposes varies little between the various groups with the exception of the unemployed. The number of residents in employment is of importance in trip generation studies because of its relationship with the work journey movement. It is closely related, however, to total resident population.

5 *Family income:* The ability to pay for a journey affects the number of trips generated by a household. Thus families with a high income can generally afford to satisfy more of their movement demands than low-income families. As one would expect, increasing family income leads to greater trip production. Family income tends to be related to levels of motor vehicle ownership.

Other factors influencing trip generation

A variety of other factors relating to the characteristics of the resident population are considered to be related to trip generation. The rateable value of a property is considered indicative of the occupiers' financial status. Thus the greater the annual outgoing in rent, or interest on invested capital, the more likely it is that the occupiers have resources available to spend on travel. Rateable value is related to family income, and because it is usually easier to obtain reliable information about rateable value than family income, rateable value is sometimes used in trip generation analysis instead of family income.

The age structure of the population is often taken into consideration in trip generation analysis on the basis that different age groups produce different movement demands and characteristics, e.g. the teenage population 15–20 years could be expected to produce more journeys of a social and recreational nature than older age groups.

83

Similarly, socio-economic characteristics of the population could be expected to produce different movement demands, e.g. blue-collar workers, i.e. factory or manual workers, could be expected to produce quite different movement characteristics to white-collar workers, i.e. executive and clerical workers. Again, preliminary work by Schuldiner has shown that trip generation analysis based on socio-economic characteristics held some promise for the future, especially in terms of a better understanding of trip length and trip interchange for the work and social trips. However, more recent work by Taylor has shown that for all modes of travel and a range of journey purposes there appears to be little relationship between the zonal socio-economic characteristics examined by him and trip generation.[4]

The degree of urbanisation exhibited by an area can be used to represent the level of integration of the household in the local community. Schuldiner derived an index of urbanisation based on fertility rate, female labour participation rate, and the incidence of single family dwellings, and found in his analysis of data relating to Chicago that it appeared to exert a significant effect on trip generation rates.[5]

Another measure of the degree of urbanisation which is often used is distance from the central area. The argument for the use of this factor is that characteristics of the population and development, and hence the movement demand, change with distance from the central area, e.g. within the central area the residential development may consist largely of 'temporary' hotel, flat and boarding-house accommodation occupied by young, single or transient persons, whilst the outer suburbs may consist largely of single family dwelling units occupied by married couples with families.

The quality of transportation facilities, and the resulting level of accessibility must affect trip generation. However, apart from preliminary work done on Accessibility Indices in North America and Europe, little is known about any relationship which might exist. Further research in this field could well result in the improvement in techniques used to predict future trip generation.

A discussion of the many variables affecting trip generation does not, however, indicate their mutual interdependence and potential use through statistical techniques for estimating trip generation. This is usually derived through multiple linear regression analysis, although more recent techniques such as category analysis have been developed to estimate future levels of trip generation.

Trip generation by multiple linear regression analysis

Multiple linear regression analysis is the statistical technique most often used to derive estimates of future trip generation, where two or more independent factors are suspected of simultaneously affecting the amount of travel. This technique measures the separate influence of each factor acting in association with other factors, and the aim of the analysis is to produce from the traffic, land-use and socio-economic data an equation of the following form

$$y = k + b_1 X_1 + b_2 X_2 + \ldots\ldots + b_n X_n$$

where y is the dependent variable (i.e. the zonal measure of traffic in terms of person movements, or movements by mode and purpose.)

X_1 to X_n are independent variables relating for example to zonal land-use, and socio-economic characteristics.

b_1 to b_n are the coefficients of the respective independent variable and k is a constant included to represent that portion of the value of y not explained by the independent variables.

In a typical regression analysis the given data relates to the present-day values of the dependent variable (y) and the independent variables (X_1 to X_n), for all the zones of the area under study. The statistical technique of 'Least Squares' fitting process is then applied to determine those values of the regression coefficients (b_1 to b_n) and the constant (k) which best fit the given data.[6,7]

The resulting regression equation is then solved using the estimated future values of the independent variables to derive the dependent variable (y—trips generated by each zone) for the appropriate target date for the study, e.g. assume that multiple linear regression analysis on present-day data derived a regression equation of the following form:

$$y = -0.59X_1 + 0.74X_2 + 0.88X_3 + -39.6X_4 + 112$$

where y = Number of work trips by all modes
      X_1 = Number of dwelling units
      X_2 = Employed persons
      X_3 = Motor vehicle ownership
      X_4 = Distance to central area

To derive an estimate of y for the target date for the study, appropriate estimates of X_1 the number of dwelling units, X_2 number of employed persons, X_3 motor vehicle ownership and X_4 distance to the central area, are substituted and the equation solved using the already established coefficients. Thus

y — number of work trips by all modes for the zone
    = $0.59 \times$ the number of dwelling units in the zone
    + $0.74 \times$ the number of employed persons in the zone
    + $0.88 \times$ the number of motor vehicles in the zone
    + $-39.6 \times$ distance to the central area
    + 112.

The quality of fit of a regression line determined by multiple linear regression analysis is indicated by the multiple correlation coefficient represented traditionally, by R. Briefly the multiple correlation coefficient takes a value between 0 and 1. The closer R is to 1 the better is the linear relationship between the variables. The closer it is to 0 the worse is the linear relationship. If the coefficient of multiple correlation is 1 the correlation is called perfect. Although a correlation coefficient of 0 indicates no linear relationship between the variables, it is possible that a non-linear relationship might exist. The significance of R is that its square (R^2) is approximately the decimal fraction of the variation in the dependent variable (y) which is accounted for by the independent variables (X_1 to X_n). Thus a multiple correlation coefficient of 0.9 indicates that approximately eight-tenths (or 80%) of the variation of the dependent variable y is explained by the independent variables included in the regression equation.

One further statistic—the standard error of estimate—is

usually derived to assess the value of the regression equation for prediction purposes. This statistic is sometimes referred to as the root mean square error, or the residual standard deviation, and is comparable statistically to the standard deviation of a group of values about their mean. It compares the quality of predicted data for the present-day situation with the observed data used to derive the regression equation and is calculated from

$$S.E.E. = \frac{\sqrt{\Sigma(Y - Y_{est})^2}}{N}$$

where S.E.E. = standard error of estimate.

Y = observed data used to derive regression equation, e.g. total work journey movements from zone A by all modes.

Y_{est} = value of Y calculated from the regression equation, e.g. estimated total work journey movements from zone A by all modes.

N = Total number of zones used in the study.

The S.E.E. (standard error of estimate) is a number which is the amount by which two-thirds of the estimated values of the dependent variable depart, either plus or minus from the observed values. Put another way, if two planes are constructed parallel to the regression plane at respective vertical distances of one, two and three standard deviations from it, then there would be included between those planes about 68%, 95% and 99·7% of the actual values.

A general measure of the value of the regression equation is the standard error of estimate as a percentage of the mean value of the dependent variables, e.g.

$$\frac{\text{Numerical S.E.E.}}{\substack{\text{Average number of} \\ \text{trips generated} \\ \text{per zone}}} \times 100$$

A good equation has a standard error of estimate which is a small percentage of the mean, and *vice versa*.

Trip generation in Cardiff[8]

A recent example illustrates the application of multiple linear regression analysis to the trip generation procedures adopted as part of the transportation planning process. In outline:

1 The over-all design of the study dictated that separate forecasts of person trips and commercial vehicle trips had to be made, and these were to be assigned to the network on a 24-hour basis.

2 To accommodate at the distribution stage trips which were not reversible it was necessary to forecast both trip productions and trip attractions for each zone. In addition, since person trips with different trip purposes display different distribution and modal split characteristics, trips were stratified by purpose throughout the forecasting stage, and separate trip generation analyses were undertaken for seven trip purposes, viz. home-based trips   1–3   from home to work, to shop and to other

           4   from work to home
           5   from shop to home
           6   from other to home

      Non-home-based trips

           7   from non-home to non-home

3 Prior to regression analysis the multiplicity of land-use and socio-economic characteristics were rationalised, and only those which could be forecast with any degree of accuracy were selected—twenty in all. These were further reduced following statistical tests, so that only those variables which could be shown to be statistically significant were included in the final regression analysis.

4 In the analysis of trip production from home seven independent variables were included in the analysis. They were:

Population
Population three years of age and over
Number of households
Number of employed residents
Number of cars owned
Area of residential land
Distance from central area

Using a step-wise regression analysis, whereby variables

which do not accord with the required level of significance are successively deleted from the equation, the above seven variables were reduced to five—the eliminated variables being population of three years of age and over, and distance to the central area. All of the remaining five variables were used in the final analysis for trip generation by purpose. However, those not reaching the required level of significance were eliminated. The resultant trip production equations for the trips from home by purpose were:

1 Trips to work $= 0.097 \times$ Zonal population
$\quad\quad\quad\quad - 351 \times$ Number of households in zone
$\quad\quad\quad\quad + 0.773 \times$ Number of employed residents
$\quad\quad\quad\quad + 0.504 \times$ Number of cars owned
$\quad\quad\quad\quad - 43.6$

R(multiple correlation coefficient) 0.99

2 Trips to shop $= 0.266 \times$ Number of cars owned
$\quad\quad\quad\quad + 1.19 \times$ Area of residential land
$\quad\quad\quad\quad - 17.9$

$R = 0.95$

3 Trips to other $= 0.086 \times$ Zonal population
$\quad\quad\quad\quad + 1.5 \times$ Number of cars owned
$\quad\quad\quad\quad - 10.1$

$R = 0.99$

5 Trip production at the non-home end. To take account of the different generation characteristics of the central area this part of the analysis considered central area and non-central area generation separately. The land-use parameters used in the initial regression analysis were numbers in employment in

Manufacturing industry
Service industry
Retail distribution
Government offices
Other offices
Wholesale distribution
Total zone employment
Area of service industry land in acres
Area of retail land (acres)
Number of households

After the initial analysis five of the above variables were selected for the more detailed analysis. They were numbers in manufacturing industry, retail employment, and total employment; the area of retail land and numbers of households.

The final regression equations for trip productions at the non-home end were as follows:

Trips from work $= +0.784 \times$ Zonal population
$+38.5$
$R = 0.97$

Trips from shopping $= +0.375 \times$ Numbers in retail employment
$+51.19 \times$ Area of retail land
$+0.032 \times$ Number of households
-1.7
$R = 0.77$

Trips from other $= -0.528 \times$ Numbers in manufacturing industry
$+0.358 \times$ Total employment
$+0.531 \times$ Number of households
$+231.1$
$R = 0.77$

Similar equations were developed for central area trip productions, although the multiple correlation coefficient tended to be lower, ranging from 0.67 to 0.98, indicating that although the independent variables used provided the most appropriate regression equation, nevertheless they only accounted for approximately half of the value of the dependent variable.

6 The analysis of commercial vehicle trip generation was carried out in the same way as that for person trips, although only one equation was developed for productions and attractions for each of the two vehicle types, i.e. light and heavy commercial vehicles. Five independent variables were found to be significant in determining the generation of commercial vehicle trips. They were total employment, office employment, retail employment, industrial employment, and numbers of households.

The two equations developed were:

Light commercial
vehicle trips $= +0.367 \times$ Number of households
$+0.267 \times$ Total employment
$-0.339 \times$ Office employment
$-0.188 \times$ Industrial employment
$+75.9$

$R = 0.88$

Heavy commercial
vehicle trips $= +0.082 \times$ Numbers of households
$+0.255 \times$ Total employment
$-0.321 \times$ Office employment
$-0.288 \times$ Retail employment
$-0.156 \times$ Industrial employment
-22.2

$R = 0.84$

7 Similar regression procedures were adopted to determine appropriate equations for trip attractions to all zones. In all, thirty regression equations were used in the trip generation analysis stage of the Cardiff study, and the high correlation coefficients achieved in the analysis show quite clearly that a strong relationship exists between land-use and trip generation. However, these relationships derived are based on existing trends and characteristics, and it is tacitly assumed in the forecasting process that these relationships will not alter significantly with time. At best the application of trip generation equations to the projected future land-use situation gives only a broad estimate of future trips. They must therefore be applied carefully, and only in conjunction with considerable experience.

Problems associated with the development of linear regression models[9]

The selection and formulation of variables* is critical in the design of the trip generation model. The dependent variable

* A point variable, for example, is density, area, or rate of growth; an aggregate variable is total population. Usually a point variable has to be multiplied by some base quantity to obtain an aggregate variable.

(y) should measure adequately what is to be predicted, whilst the independent variables should provide an adequate explanation of the dependent variable as well as retaining a separate identity.

Two fundamental criteria to be adhered to in the formulation of variables are:

1 They should be of the same type, i.e. point and aggregate variables should not be mixed

2 they should be capable of clear interpretation, i.e. they must be capable of being named and measured.

Two assumptions are necessary before multiple linear regression can be applied in trip generation. They are:

1 that a linear relationship exists between the dependent and independent variables,

2 that the influence of the independent variables is additive, i.e. the inclusion of each variable contributes towards accounting for the value of the dependent variable.

It is normal practice to test for linearity of relationship between variables by plotting a sample of the relevant data on graph paper, and visually inspecting the results. If linearity does not exist then the original variables can be modified to produce a linear relationship by taking the log, square root or reciprocal of the variable, e.g. the *Cardiff Development and Transportation Study*[10] derived a regression equation to predict car ownership by using the log of income, and the log of residential density, to overcome problems associated with a non-linear relationship. The final equation took the form:

Cars per household $= -1\cdot976$
$+1\cdot03\times$log income
$-0\cdot366\times$log residential density

If two independent variables are highly interrelated they generally yield non-additive influences on the dependent variable. It is possible to test for this by carrying out tests for correlation between the independent variables suspected of having a high interrelationship. If the correlation coefficient(s) is high then it is assumed that the interrelationship between the independent variables tested is also high.

This problem can be overcome by either eliminating the

least important variable in the model, or by combining the two variables, provided the new aggregate variable can be named and measured. If all the variables must be included in the model then the statistical technique of factor analysis can be adopted to aggregate variables into independent and therefore additive influences. The basic criticisms of multiple linear regression analysis in trip generation are that (1) because it is empirical in nature it fails to establish a causal relationship between the dependent and independent variables, and (2) to use the derived equation for prediction purposes it has to be assumed that the regression coefficients established at a given time will be relevant in the future.

Category analysis[11]

In an attempt to overcome some of the problems associated with the use of multiple regression techniques to estimate future trip generation rates, 'Category Analysis' was developed and introduced in the course of the second phase of the *London Traffic Survey*. This method is based on the assumption that trip generation rates for different categories of household will remain constant in the future. Thus by knowing the generation rate for each category of household, and the number of such households for some future date, estimates of future trip generation can be successfully derived. It places each household into one of 108 categories based on locational and household characteristics. From survey data relating to present-day trip generation an average trip generation rate is established. This average rate is then used in conjunction with future estimates of the number of households in each category, thus allowing future generation rates to be estimated, for three different modes of travel (drivers, passengers and public transport) and six journey purposes (work, business, education, shopping, social, non-home-based).

The underlying assumptions of category analysis are that 1 the household as an independent unit, from which most journeys begin or end in response to the requirements of members of the family, is the fundamental unit in the trip generation process.

2 the journeys generated by the household depend on the characteristics of that household and its location relative to its required facilities such as work place and shops.

3 households with one set of characteristics produce a different average trip generation rate from households with other characteristics.

4 trip generation rates are stable over time so long as factors external to the household are the same as when the trip rates were first measured.

The 108 different categories of household are derived by considering those household characteristics most readily isolated and which are considered to be responsible for a systematic variation in trip generation. They are disposable income, levels of car ownership and family size and structure. For each characteristic a number of categories is selected, as follows:

Disposable income
1 Less than £500 p.a.
2 £500 to £1,000
3 £1,000 to £1,500
4 £1,500 to £2,000
5 £2,000 to £2,500
6 £2,500+

Car ownership
1 nil cars per household
2 1 car per household
3 2+ cars per household.

Household structure
1 No employed residents and one non-employed adult.
2 No employed residents and two or more non-employed adults.
3 One employed resident and one or less non-employed adults.
4 One employed resident and two or more non-employed adults.
5 Two or more employed residents and one or less non-employed adults.
6 Two or more employed residents and two or more non-employed adults.

In the original exercise consideration of the effect of the location of the household in relation to the required destination and to the existing transport facilities was attempted through the use of Bus and Rail Accessibility Indices, and the general conclusion was that such factors are of secondary importance in trip generation. However, the indices measured were crude in form, and it is possible that the use of more sophisticated indices might have revealed a stronger relationship between trip generation and locational qualities.

Conclusion

Reliable short-term estimates of future trip generation rates have been derived by multiple linear regression analysis. Similarly it would seem that a comparable degree of accuracy will be achieved through category analysis. For the long term it is impossible to say at this stage if both, or either, will give acceptable predictions.

The fundamental weakness associated with multiple linear regression analysis is that it fails to establish a causal relationship between the dependent and independent variables, and assumes that regression coefficients established today will hold good for any future date. Both assumptions are questionable. An empirical examination of the current relationships between traffic and certain land-use/socio-economic factors may show a high degree of correlation which results from a peculiar set of present-day conditions rather than through any causal relationship. Thus given changing circumstances with time the degree of correlation could be reduced to negligible proportions, with the result that predictions based on the original regression equation could be inaccurate. Similarly, changes in the land-use and socio-economic characteristics could result in a different relationship between the independent variables expressed in terms of completely different regression coefficients. Again, predictions based on the original regression equation could give wildly inaccurate results.

Category analysis, which bases its predictions on the assumption that the trip generation rates exhibited today by different classes of household will hold good in the future, avoids these criticisms, and holds much promise for further research and development. However, the problems associated with predicting accurately on a zonal basis for some future date, the number of households in each of the 108 categories, are considerable.

References

1 Corradino J. C., The effect of the highway system and land development on trip production, *Traffic Engineering* (1968).
2 Buchanan Colin and Partners, *Traffic in Guildford* (1965).
3 Schuldiner P. W., Trip Generation and the Home; *Highway Research Board*, Bulletin No. 347 (1962).
4 Taylor M. A., Studies of travel in Gloucester, *Northampton and Reading, Road Research Laboratory Report*, No. LR 141 (Tables 55 and 57).
5 Schuldiner P. W., *op.cit.*
6 For an easily understood explanation of the statistical procedures involved in correlation and multiple linear regression analysis see: Spiegel M. R., *Theory and Outline of Statistics*, Schaums Outline Series, McGraw-Hill (pp. 240–280), (1961).
7 For an explanation of the theory and application of correlation and multiple linear regression analysis see: Johnston J., *Econometric Methods*, McGraw-Hill (1961).
8 Buchanan Colin and Partners in association with Atkins W. S., *Cardiff Development and Transportation Study*, Main Study Report, Supplementary Technical Volume No 5.
9 Hill D. M. and Brand D., Methodology for developing activity distribution models by linear regression analysis, *Highway Research Board*, Record No. 126 (1966).
10 Buchanan Colin and Partners, *Cardiff Development and Transportation Study* (as above).
11 Wootton H. J. and Pick G. W., A model for trips generated by households, *Journal of Transport Economics and Policy* (1967).

4　Trip distribution

Introduction

Trip distribution, or in American terminology 'interzonal transfers', is that part of the transportation planning process which relates a given number of travel origins for every zone of the area under study, to a given number of travel destinations located within the other zones of the area. It is not necessarily concerned with the mode of travel used for a given trip, nor the routes which could be taken to complete this trip. Rather it is concerned with establishing the links between a number of zones for which trip generation calculations have previously been made.

During the past two decades various mathematical procedures have been developed and used for this purpose, and they tend to fall into two main groups.

1 Analogous or growth factor methods—in which growth factors are applied to present-day interzonal movements.

2 Synthetic﹒ or 'inter-area travel formulae'—in which an attempt is made to understand the causal relationship behind patterns of movement, by assuming them to be similar to certain laws of physical behaviour. Once understood, these causal relationships are projected into the future and the appropriate travel pattern is synthesised.

Despite the diversity of formulation used in the various

mathematical procedures developed, the underlying principle in all trip distribution models is the same:

'Travel between any two points will increase with increase of attraction for such travel, but decrease as the resistance to travel increases.'[1]

Growth factor methods

Four different growth factor methods of trip distribution have been developed, each based on the assumption that present travel patterns can be projected into the future, using expected differential zonal rates of growth. This group of methods can be represented in general terms by the formula

$$T_{i-j} = t_{i-j}E$$

T_{i-j}—Future number of trips from zone i to zone j
t_{i-j}—Existing number of trips from zone i to zone j
E—Growth Factor.

Depending on the method used the growth factor (E) can be a single factor, or a combination of several factors, derived from land use and trip generation projections. It can be calculated for the area as a whole, or for any number of zones within it, and is then applied to a complete origin and destination matrix for the study area.

The four growth factor methods in chronological order of their development are

1 Uniform factor
2 Average factor
3 Fratar
4 Detroit

1 *Uniform factor*

The uniform factor is the oldest and simplest method of projecting future trip distribution. A single growth factor is calculated for the entire area under study, and this is used to multiply all existing interzonal movements to produce estimates of future interzonal movements.

98

Mathematically this can be expressed as

$$T_{i-j} = t_{i-j} E$$

where $E = \dfrac{T}{t}$

T_{i-j} = Future number of trips from zone i to zone j

t_{i-j} = Present number of trips from zone i to zone j

T = Total future number of trips in the area under study

t = Total present number of trips in the area under study

The basic assumption behind the uniform factor method is that the expected growth in the area as a whole will exert the same influence on the growth of movements between any pair of zones located within it. However, this assumption is not strictly correct, for differential rates of urban development inevitably result in different rates of growth in movement. Thus in those zones where present-day development is limited, the potential changes in the pattern, density and type of land use are such that the application of a uniform growth factor to the existing volume of movements, would lead to an under-estimation of future movements. Similarly, it could lead to an overestimation of movement volumes in those areas which are already intensively developed.

For this reason the method is now only used to update the results of recent origin and destination surveys in areas where the pattern and intensity of land uses are relatively stable.

2 *Average factor*

The average factor method was an early attempt to take some account of the differential rates of growth of movement which occur in urban areas. It utilises a growth factor for each zone within the study area which, like the uniform factor method, is derived from land use and trip generation predictions. Mathematically it can be expressed:

$$T_{i-j} = t_{i-j} \frac{(E_i + E_j)}{2}$$

99

where $E_i = \dfrac{T_i}{t_i}$ and $E_j = \dfrac{T_j}{t_j}$

    T_{i-j} = Future number of trips from zone i to zone j
    t_{i-j} = Present number of trips from zone i to zone j
E_i and E_j = Growth factors for zones i and j
  T_i, T_j = Future movements originating in i or destined for j
  t_i, t_j = Present movements originating in i, or destined for j

In general, the calculated values will not give total flows originating or terminating in a zone which agree with future estimates derived from the trip generation analysis. That is

$$T_i \neq T_{i(G)}$$

where $T_i = \displaystyle\sum_{j=1}^{n} T_{i-j}$ = Total calculated flows originating in zone i

and $T_{i(G)}$ = Trip generation estimates for total flows originating in zone i.

This discrepancy can be reduced by an iterative process which uses the estimates of future traffic flows derived from the trip generation stage ($T_{i(G)}$) and those computed from the first application of the average factor (T_i) to calculate new growth factors, which are then applied to the estimated flows, as computed from the first application of the average factor method (T_{i-j}). Thus

$$E_i{}^1 = \frac{T_{i(G)}}{T_i}$$

$$E_j{}^1 = \frac{T_{j(G)}}{T_j}.$$

and for the first iteration

$$T_{i-j}{}^1 = T_{i-j} \cdot \frac{(E_i{}^1 + E_j{}^1)}{2}$$

The process of iteration is continued until the new growth factors approximate to unity and T_i converges to $T_{i(G)}$.

Criticism levelled at the uniform factor method are also applicable to the average factor method. In addition, the residual discrepancies between forecasted and computed trips are not randomly distributed, but are inversely related to the growth factors. Thus for zones with lower than average growth factors, computed trip ends are greater than those originally predicted from the trip generation stage, whilst the reverse applies for those zones with higher than average growth factors.[2] This bias declines with each succeeding iteration, but if a large number of iterations is required to minimise this bias the accuracy of the results may be seriously affected. For this reason the average factor method is only rarely used today.

An interesting approach in the use of the growth factor technique in trip distribution is the method developed by W. S. Pollard Jr,[3] whereby human judgement is used in conjunction with the mechanical methods outlined above. Basically the method adopted by him involves the application of a growth factor to existing interzonal movements. This factor is an average of the growth factors of each pair of zones involved unless the circumstances relating to one or both of the zones requires an adjustment to be made to the growth factor. The application of these adjustments to secure a balance in the trip distribution process requires time, and needs to be guided by 'sound judgement, intimate local planning and engineering knowledge'.[4] The fact that the adjustments can only be made after the movement concerned has been extensively studied would seem to rule it out as a practicable method of forecasting trip distribution in the urban transportation study, where many thousands of different movements must be catered for.

3 Fratar

T. J. Fratar, whilst working on travel forecasts for the Cleveland (Ohio) Metropolitan Region, used the process of iteration to develop a trip distribution method which overcomes the disadvantages associated with the uniform and average factor methods. The assumptions basic to his method are that (a) the distribution of future trips from a given zone of origin is proportional to the present trip distribution from that zone and (b) the distribution of these future trips is modified by the growth factor of the zone to which these trips are attracted.

This modification takes into account the effect of the location of a given zone with respect to all other zones, and is expressed as the reciprocal of the average attracting 'pull' of all these other zones. Broadly the method formulated involves:

1 the estimation of the total number of trips which are expected to originate and terminate in each traffic zone at the date for which trip distribution is required. (This is carried out at the trip generation stage.)

2 The distribution of future trip ends from each zone to all the other zones in the study area, in proportion to the present distribution of trips, modified by the growth factor of the zone to which the trips are attracted. This yields two values for each interzonal movement $(i—j$ and $j—i)$, and an average of these values is taken as the first approximation of the interzonal volumes.

3 For each zone the sum of the first approximation volumes is divided into the total volume desired for the zone, as estimated from the trip generation stage, to derive the new growth factor to be used in computing the second approximation.

4 The estimated interzonal trips for each zone in the first approximation are again distributed, in proportion to the present interzonal volumes and the new growth factor obtained in the first approximation. The pairs of values derived are again averaged and the process repeated until the conformity between calculated and 'desired' trips is achieved.

Mathematically, the Fratar method can be expressed as

$$T_{i-j} = \frac{T_{i(G)} \; t_{i-j} \; E_j}{t_{i-j} \; E_j + t_{i-k} \; E_k + \ldots\ldots + t_{i-n} \; E_n}$$

where $\quad T_{i-j}$ = Predicted number of trips zone $i—j$

$\qquad T_{i(G)}$ = Expected future number of trips generated from zone i

$t_{i-j}\ldots\ldots t_{i-n}$ = Present number of trips between zone i and all other zones $j\ldots\ldots n$

$E_i\ldots\ldots E_n$ = Growth factors of individual zones $i\ldots\ldots n$

The process of iteration necessary to produce a balance between the number of predicted trips (T_{i-j}) and the number of expected trips $T_{i(G)}$ is fairly complicated and laborious.

It is best illustrated by the example used by Fratar in explaining the method.[5]

The following present-day interzonal movements are assumed

Zones	A	B	C	D
A	—	10	12	18
B	10	—	14	14
C	12	14	—	6
D	18	14	6	—
Total	40	38	32	38
Future trips generated ($T_{i\,(G)}$—estimated from trip generation analysis)	80	114	48	38
First approximation growth factors	2	3	1·5	1

Thus from zone A the future total trips (80) would be distributed between zones A–B, A–C, A–D in proportion to the present-day interzonal movements, modified by the expected growth of the destination zones.

Thus
$$T_{A-B} = \frac{80 \times 10 \times 3}{(10 \times 3) + (12 \times 1\cdot5) + (18 \times 1)} = 36\cdot4$$

and
$$T_{B-A} = \frac{114 \times 10 \times 2}{(10 \times 2) + (14 \times 1\cdot5) + (14 \times 1)} = 41\cdot5$$

The average of these two values is then taken as the first approximation of future interzonal movements A–B, i.e. 39.

The same procedure is followed for all combinations of movements, A–B, A–C, A–D, B–C, B–D, C–D, which produces a table (top of p. 104) for the first approximation of future interzonal trips.

	A–B	A–C	A–D	B–C	B–D	C–D
	36·4	21·8	21·8	43·5	29·0	3·9
	41·5	16·0	15·8	28·0	18·3	4·0
Total	77·9	37·8	37·6	71·5	47·3	7·9
Average first approximation	39·0	18·9	18·8	35·7	23·6	4·0

The averages for the trips generated from each zone are summarised, related to the expected volumes and the new growth factor calculated.

	A	B	C	D
	39·0	39·0	18·9	18·8
	18·9	35·7	35·7	23·6
	18·8	23·6	4·0	4·0
New totals	76·7	98·3	58·6	46·4
Expected volumes $(T_{i\,(G)})$	80·0	114·0	48·0	38·0
New growth factor	1·04	1·16	0·82	0·82

This process is repeated, using the new growth factor with the matrix formed with the values of the first approximation, until the required balance is achieved.

A modification of the Fratar method was suggested by the Urban Planning division of the United States Bureau of Public Roads, in 1962, to consider up to ten different trip purposes, and to apply growth factors by mode, time of day, or separately for trips entering or leaving a zone. This modification results in the method becoming much more sensitive to any land-use changes that might occur in a given zone. However, this advantage is offset by the fact that the modification complicates even further an already involved method.

4 Detroit

The Detroit method of trip distribution was developed in connection with the Detroit Metropolitan Area Traffic Study, in an attempt to overcome the shortcomings of the simpler growth factors, whilst at the same time reducing the computer operations necessary to bring the Fratar method to a satisfactory balance.[6] It is similar in approach to the average factor and Fratar methods, but introduces the assumption that although the number of trips generated in zone i will increase as predicted by the appropriate growth factor E_i, these will be distributed to zone j in proportion to the appropriate growth factor E_j divided by the growth factor for the area as a whole. Thus:

$$T_{i-j} = t_{i-j} \frac{E_i \times E_j}{E}$$

where T_{i-j}=Predicted future trips from zone i to zone j
$\qquad t_{i-j}$=Existing number of trips from zone i to zone j
$\quad E_i$, E_j=Growth factors for zones i and j
$\qquad E$=Growth factor for the area as a whole

As with the Fratar method the computed trip ends (T_{i-j}) for any zone will generally not equal the forecasted trip ends for that zone $T_{i-j(G)}$. Iteration is therefore necessary to bring the results into balance and the new growth factors E_i^1 and E_j^1 are computed using the ratio of the computed and forecasted trip ends. Thus

$$E_i^1 = \frac{T_{i(G)}}{T_i}$$

$T_{i(G)}$=forecasted trip ends in zone i from trip generation stage
$\quad T_i$=computed trip ends in zone i

The growth factors used in the Detroit method are much simpler to calculate than the complicated factors used in the Fratar method.

Conclusions

The main advantages associated with the growth factor method of trip distribution are that

1 they are easily understood and applied; requiring only an inventory of the present-day trip origins and destinations, and an estimation of simple growth factors

2 the simple process of iteration quickly produces a balance between postulated $(T_{i(G)})$ and computed (T_i) trip ends

3 they are flexible in application and can be used to distribute trips by different modes, for different purposes, at different times of the day, and can be applied to directional flows

4 they have been well tested and have been found to be accurate when applied to areas where the pattern and density of development is stable.

These advantages are, however, outweighed by the problems associated with their application. Because they require as input data the results of a comprehensive Origin and Destination survey, they are expensive to apply. They cannot be used to predict travel patterns in areas where significant changes in land use are likely to occur, and the assumption that the present day travel resistance factors will remain constant into the future is fundamentally weak.

Because the chances of statistical error are greater, the application of a growth factor to small present-day interzonal movements can result in extremely unreliable estimates of future movements. Zonal growth factors are derived after a process of crude approximation, yet the growth factor method of distribution relies on their accurate determination. Trips which have their destination in their zone of origin are automatically excluded from the growth factor method of distribution, and this results in errors, and increases the need for iteration which itself gives rise to the possibility of creating more errors.

For short-term predictions in stable areas, or for updating recent Origin and Destination survey data, these methods can be used with success. However, they cannot satisfy the requirements of modern urban transportation studies, which are usually designed to cater for conditions of continual and rapid change in the patterns of development, and the way of life of the population generally.

Synthetic methods

The fundamental shortcomings associated with the use of growth factor methods of trip distribution were identified in the early stages of their development, with the result that research work concentrated on the development of alternative methods, as well as the improvement of the growth factor techniques. The most successful alternatives—now generally referred to as the synthetic methods—were based on the assumption that (1) before future travel patterns can be predicted, the underlying causes of movement must first be understood; (2) the causal relationships giving rise to movement patterns can best be understood if they are considered to be similar to certain laws of physical behaviour.

Basically these synthetic methods include the gravity model, the opportunity model, the multiple regression model, and the electrostatic model. The first three methods analyse present-day travel pattern data, to establish relationships between the number of trips made between each pair of zones; the attractiveness of the zone of attraction, and the resistance to travel that exists between each pair of zones.

1 *Gravity model method*

The gravity model is perhaps the most widely used synthetic method of trip distribution, because it is simple to understand and apply, and is well documented. It adapts the concept of gravity as advanced by Newton in 1686 and is based on the assumption that trip interchange between zones is directly proportional to the relative attraction of each zone and inversely proportional to some function of the spatial separation between zones. In mathematical terms the gravity model is expressed

$$T_{i-j} = P_i \frac{\dfrac{A_j}{(D_{i-j})^b}}{\dfrac{A_j}{(D_{i-j})^b} + \dfrac{A_k}{(D_{i-k})^b} + \cdots\cdots + \dfrac{A_n}{(D_{i-n})^b}}$$

where T_{i-j}=Number of trips produced in zone i with a destination in zone j

P_i=Total number of trips produced in zone i

A_j=Total Number of trips attracted to zone j

$D_{i-j}...D_{i-n}$=measure of spatial separation between zones $i-j......i-n$

b=Empirically determined exponent which expresses the average area wide effect of spatial separation between zones on trip interchange.

1 *Development of the gravity model:* The early gravity model had its origins in sociological studies. In 1929, W. J. Reilly developed a simple gravity model in an attempt to analyse and understand the pattern of retail trade areas associated with different towns. His 'law' stated that:

'Two cities attract retail trade, primarily shopping goods, from an intermediate city or town . . . approximately in direct proportion to the population of the two cities, and in inverse proportion to the square of the distances from these two cities to the intermediate town.'[7]

The first real application of the gravity model technique to transportation planning came when Reilly's Law was adapted by H. J. Casey Jr to allocate to any number of 'towns' the purchases of any number of 'intermediate' towns.[8] Basically this adaptation states 'the purchases of the residents of a neighbourhood . . . are attracted to the retail centres in direct proportion to the size of the centres and inversely as the squares of the driving time distances from the neighbourhood to the retail centre'. Mathematically this is expressed

$$B_{i-a}=\left[\frac{\frac{F_a}{(D_{i-a})^2}}{\frac{F_a}{(D_{i-a})^2}+\frac{F_b}{(D_{i-b})^2}+...+\frac{F_n}{(D_{i-n})^2}}\right]\times B_i$$

where B_{i-a}=Purchases made by residents of neighbourhood i in shopping centre a

$$B_i = \text{'Buying power' of neighbourhood } i$$

$$F_a, F_b, F_c...F_n = \text{Amount of retail floor space in shopping centres } a, b, c,...n$$

$$D_{i-a}...D_{i-n} = \text{Driving time distances between neighbourhood } i \text{ and competing shopping centres } a, b, c...n$$

Further research by Voohees showed that although the principle of the law of gravity could be used with advantage in trip distribution, the measure of attractiveness of a zone of attraction, and the exponent of the distance factor, varied with the purpose of the journey being undertaken. Thus the basic formula, derived by Casey, was re-written to distribute work journey trips

$$W_{i-a} = \left[\frac{\dfrac{E_a}{\sqrt{D_{i-a}}}}{\dfrac{E_a}{\sqrt{D_{i-a}}} + \dfrac{E_b}{\sqrt{D_{i-b}}} + ... + \dfrac{E_n}{\sqrt{D_{i-n}}}} \right] \times W_i$$

where W_{i-a} = Number of work journeys from neighbourhood i to work zone a

W_i = Total number of workers resident in neighbourhood i

$E_a, E_b...E_n$ = Total number of jobs in work zones $a, b,...n$

$D_{i-a}...D_{i-n}$ = driving time distance between neighbourhood i and work zones $a, b,...n$

Voorhees found that the most satisfactory measure of attractiveness of the work zones was the total number of persons employed; and that the most appropriate exponent of the distance factor was $\frac{1}{2}$. Similarly, Voorhees found that when distributing social trips the exponent of the distance factor was 3 (D^3), and when distributing shopping trips the exponent was 2 (D^2).

This relatively simple gravity model was a major breakthrough in the field of trip distribution. It stressed the importance of specific values of trip attraction and resistance, and recognised the influence of trip purpose on travel patterns. It could be used with advantage over the growth factor methods in that changes in the future land-use pattern could now be accounted for, and that improvements to existing transportation facilities could be taken into consideration in the travel-resistance factor.

Despite these advantages two major shortcomings were associated with this simple gravity model: (1) the inverse power of distance was an unsatisfactory resistance function because it could not cover the full range of trip possibilities and failed to give valid estimates when the distance factor was very small or very large; (2) the comprehensive iteration process required to calibrate the model, allied to the number of trip purposes used as input and the variations in travel with zonal location that had to be accounted for, gave rise to serious computational problems.

Consequently, a more efficient form of resistance function, known as travel-time factors, was developed to express the effect of spatial separation on zonal trip interchanges. The use of these factors greatly simplifies the computational processes involved in applying the model, and also takes into account the fact that the effect of spatial separation on trip making increases in a much more complex way than can be represented by a single exponent.

2 *The gravity model today:* To take account of these travel-time factors, the basic gravity model formula is modified. Thus

$$T_{i-j} = \frac{P_i \, A_j \, F_{i-j} \, K_{i-j}}{\sum\limits_{j=1}^{n} A_j \, F_{i-j} \, K_{i-j}}$$

where T_{i-j} = Number of trips from zone i–j

P_i = Total number of trips produced in zone i

A_j = Total number of trips attracted to zone j

F_{i-j} = Empirically derived travel-time factor expressing the average area-wide effect of spatial separation

K_{i-j} = Specific zone to zone adjustment factor to account for other social and economic factors influencing travel pattern but not accounted for in the model.

In effect the travel-time factors are a measure of the probability of trip making at each chosen increment of travel time. They are empirically derived through a 'trial and error' process, and the usual procedure is to start with the adoption of a set of travel-time factors already calculated for a similar town (an alternative is to assume that travel time has no effect on trip distribution and adopt 1 as the first travel-time factor). The next step involves the calculation of zonal interchanges using the gravity model (T_{i-j}), which are then compared with the present-day zonal interchanges derived from the O–D survey (t_{i-j}). An iteration process is adopted until there is close agreement between the two sets of zonal interchanges. Generally it is accepted that satisfactory agreement is reached when the difference between average trip lengths is $\pm 3\%$, and trip length frequency curves are 'close' when compared visually.

Mathematically, iteration is achieved by

$$F_{i-j}{}^1 = F_{i-j} \times \frac{t_{i-j}}{T_{i-j}}$$

where $F_{i-j}{}^1$ = Travel-time factor to be used in the next step of the procedure

F_{i-j} = Travel-time factor adopted from similar town, (or assumed 1).

T_{i-j} = Trips i–j as a percentage of total trips calculated from gravity model.

t_{i-j} = trips i–j as a percentage of total present-day trips derived from O–D survey

In addition to the travel-time factors incorporated in the gravity model used today, provision is also made for the inclusion of zone to zone socio-economic adjustment factors (K_{i-j}), should they prove necessary for the successful calibration of the model. Experience has shown that these factors are not usually necessary in smaller towns of less than 100,000 population. However, there are occasions when they have to be used in the larger urban areas to produce satisfactory trip distribution results, and eliminate any systematic errors which might occur.

The procedure adopted to calculate the socio-economic adjustment factor is to compare the estimated trip interchanges between large generators of movement, using the gravity model (T_{i-j}) with the observed present-day interchanges

(t_{i-j}). Both sets of movements are manually assigned to a transport network, to reveal any systematic discrepancies.[9] Mathematically the adjustment factor (K_{i-j}) is derived from

$$K_{i-j} = R_{i-j} \frac{1 - X_i}{1 - X_i R_{i-j}}$$

where R_{i-j} = Ratio of $O-D$ trip interchanges t_{i-j}, to gravity model trip interchanges T_{i-j}

X_i = Ratio of $O-D$ trips $i-j$ to total $O-D$ trips leaving zone i

Conclusions: The gravity model is easy to understand and use. It recognises that trip purpose is a major influence in determining travel patterns, and accounts for the competition which exists between different land uses. Any changes in travel-time between zones can be readily taken into account, whilst the use of an adjustment factor ensures that socio-economic factors can be accommodated if necessary.

The basic operational difficulty associated with the use of the gravity model is that it requires a considerable amount of adjustment and manipulation to achieve satisfactory results. This can be taken as an indication that the gravity model procedure allows a sufficient number of adjustments to be made to the model so that the existing travel pattern is accurately reproduced, without adequately representing the relationships underlying these movements. There is no guarantee that present-day travel time and socio-economic factors will remain constant up to the design year.

2 The 'electrostatic field' method

In an attempt to overcome the need for expensive $O-D$ surveys R. T. Howe developed a model to distribute person movements, based on Coulomb's Law of Electrostatic Force. His model

'... considers human beings as electronics. Given the initial distribution of these unit negative charges corresponding to centres of residence, and the distribution of centres of positive charge, representing places of employment, with magnitudes equalling the number of persons employed, the probability of movements between place of residence and places of employment can be predicted on the basis of the electrostatic field theory.'[10]

The first stage in the development of the model involved the consideration of work journey movements only, and made the following assumptions:

1 the area under examination is a closed system, i.e. every worker lives and works within the same area, and every job within the area is filled by a worker resident in the area.

2 the work journey movement pattern is stable, i.e. every worker travels to work every day.

3 the employment structure is balanced throughout the area, i.e. no unusual concentrations of a particular type of employee exist.

4 all income levels are evenly distributed throughout all the residential zones in the area.

5 the spatial separation between zones of residence and employment is measured by the straight line distance.

6 movement occurs within the system because of the initial imbalance between positive charges (jobs) and negative charges (people).

From the original hypothesis, and using the assumptions outlined above, Howe, in a study of the work trips in the Minneapolis–St. Paul area, developed two equations to distribution person movements:

1
$$V_{P_i Q_j} = \frac{\dfrac{Q_j}{R_{ij}} P_i}{\displaystyle\sum_{j=1}^{m} \dfrac{Q_j}{R_{ij}}} \quad (i = 1, 2, \ldots\ldots n)$$

2
$$V_{Q_j P_i} = \frac{\dfrac{P_i}{R_{ij}} Q_j}{\displaystyle\sum_{i=1}^{n} \dfrac{P_i}{R_{ij}}} \quad (j = 1, 2, \ldots\ldots n)$$

where $V_{P_iQ_j}$=Probability of movement from zone i to zone j
P_i=Number of workers living in zone i
Q_j=Number of jobs available in zone j
R_{ij}=Straightline distance from zone i to zone j
$V_{Q_jP_i}$=Probability of movement from zone j to zone i

Equation 1 ensures that the correct number of workers is drawn from each zone of residence. Equation 2 ensures that the correct number of workers is assigned to each employment zone. However, the two equations yield different sets of movements, with the result that to avoid under or over assignment of person movements to the different traffic zones, a balancing process using correction factors must be undertaken.

Following his analysis of the work journey movements, Howe extended his theory to include shopping trips. Based on similar assumptions, the whole theory was again extensively tested against 1957 O–D data from the Cedar Rapids–Mario area, Iowa, and similar equations derived.

The electrostatic field method by Howe is similar in form to the early gravity models. The advantages claimed for it are that the method is simple and inexpensive to apply. The future pattern of movements can be predicted without analysing the existing movements. Information relating to the numbers and locations of workers and jobs, and the straight line distance between zones is all that is required for the process to be set in motion.

The disadvantages associated with the method are that it can only deal with a closed system. It cannot simulate movements across an external cordon. In addition the similarity of the model to the early gravity models implies that it has the same shortcomings as those models although no attempt is made to overcome these shortcomings by the introduction of adjusting factors.

3 The multiple regression method

The multiple regression method is an empirical approach to determine from Origin and Destination and land-use/planning data the socio-economic variables that are the best predictors of trip distribution. It was first developed by Sam Osofsky in California, in connection with a research project to find 'a reliable, logical and practical method of developing data to be used in designing and locating freeways of the future'.[11]

The project utilised data collected in the *San Diego Home Interview Study*, and as a first stage plotted as the dependent variable, the number of trips from a specific zone to all other zones, against four independent variables known to be significantly related to trips between zones—the distance between zone centroids in miles, population, employed persons and vehicle ownership in the zone.

As a result of this exercise it was found that the number of trips between zones tends to increase with an increase in zonal populations, employed persons and car ownership, and decrease with increasing distance between zone centroids. However, no clear-cut relationship which related to all the zones within the study area was established.

The next stage in the research project was the consideration of a multiple regression approach, which was based on the assumption that trip distribution is inversely proportional to the distance between zones, and is directly proportional to the population, employment, car ownership and land use of each zone. A number of trial regression equations were developed for the Modesto and Sacramento area, and the method adapted involved

1 the selection of an appropriate equation form, determined from experience and theory

2 the calculation of a set of co-efficients relating a specific zone to all other zones. These co-efficients were derived from origin and destination and land-use/planning data, and the process was repeated treating each zone in turn as a specific zone, until a set of co-efficients was derived for each zone and cordon station.

3 the estimation of the 'theoretical' trips at the survey period, using the same independent variables, and the co-efficients derived above.

4 the comparison of existing interzonal movements and theoretical trip distribution to check that the original equation form was sound.

5 the projection of the independent variables to the design year.

6 the calculation of future trip distribution in the design year using the projected independent variables from 5 above and the co-efficients calculated in 2 above.

i.e. Mathematically an equation of the form

$$t_{i-j} = a_0 + a_1 x_1 + a_2 x_2 + \ldots\ldots + a_n x_n$$

is determined for each zone, to explain the present-day movements, using the method of least squares.

To forecast future movements a similar equation is developed of the form

$$T_{i-j} = a_0 + a_1 X_1 + a_2 X_2 + \ldots\ldots + a_n X_n$$

where t_{i-j} = Present-day movements from zone i–j

a_0 = Constant

$a_1 - a_n$ = Co-efficients determined by method of least squares

$x_1 - x_n$ = Present-day values for independent variables, e.g. population, car ownership

and T_{i-j} = Predicted trips i–j for the design year.

$X_1 - X_n$ = Predicted values for design year of same independent variables, i.e. population, car ownership

The final equation developed by Osofsky took the form

$$T_{i-j} = a_1 \frac{P^2}{D^{1.5}} + a_2 \frac{E^2}{D^{1.5}} + a_3 \frac{V}{D^{1.5}} + a_4 \frac{L}{D^{1.5}} + a_0$$

where P = Population in each destination zone

E = Employed persons in each destination zone

V = Vehicle ownership in each destination zone

L = Land-use index for each destination zone

D = Distance

As part of the project the multiple regression method of trip distribution was compared with a gravity model method, and it was found that the root-mean-square error* was considerably less for the multiple regression model.

* Root-mean-square error—see page 87 of Chapter 3, *Trip Generation* for explanation.

As a method of forecasting future trip distribution the multiple regression model has several distinct advantages. Unlike the gravity model it can include in the equation any variable thought to have an influence on trip distribution. It is easy to understand and it can be applied to any area for any trip purpose. One underlying weakness however is the assumption that the relationship between trip volumes and the independent variables (i.e. the co-efficients $a_0, a,...a_n$) remains constant from the present time to the design year.

4 The 'opportunities' methods

There are two basic 'opportunities' methods of distributing future movements. (*a*) The intervening opportunities model and (*b*) the competing opportunities model. Both methods introduce the theory of probability as the theoretical foundation on which the trip distribution is based, and were developed as the result of research undertaken in connection with the Chicago, Pittsburgh and Penn–Jersey transportation studies.

In essence both the opportunities models can be represented by a general formula

$$T_{i-j} = T_{i(G)} \times P_j$$

where T_{i-j} = Predicted number of trips from zone i to zone j
$T_{i(G)}$ = Total number of trips originating in zone i
P_j = Calculated probability of a trip stopping in zone j

The difference between the two opportunities methods is the way in which the probability function P_j is calculated.

1 *Intervening opportunities:* The intervening opportunities model was developed for the *Chicago Area Transportation Study* and was the first method to use the probability function to describe trip distribution in an urban area. The assumption basic to the model is that within an urban area all trips will want to remain as short as possible, lengthening only as they fail to find an acceptable destination at a shorter distance.

'... a trip prefers to remain as short as possible, but its behaviour is governed by a probability of stopping at any destination it encounters—it cannot always go to the nearest destination and stop; it must consider the nearest destination, and if that is unacceptable, consider the next nearest and so on.'[12]

It is of interest to note that this idea is similar to the physical law concerning the principles governing the distribution of lengths of path of molecules in a gas, and was first developed by S. A. Stouffer in a study of migration patterns of families in Cleveland, Ohio, in the 1930s.[13] Stouffer found that the number of people migrating a given distance was proportional to the opportunities for satisfaction at that distance and inversely proportional to the number of intervening opportunities.

A simple example, taken from the *Report of the Chicago Area Transportation Study*[14] illustrates the principles involved in the application of this idea to the distribution of movements. Assume that

1 within an urban area, one destination in every one hundred destinations sells milk

2 of those destinations which sell milk, only every second one sells 'brand X'.

In the above situation the probability that a randomly chosen destination within this area will satisfy a hypothetical movement wishing to obtain brand X is:

$$\frac{1}{100} \times \frac{1}{2} = \frac{1}{200}$$

i.e. the person has a 1 in 200 chance of obtaining brand X at his first destination, and therefore a 199 in 200 chance of going on to the next destination. The chances of this person stopping at the second destination are the chances of his having got there (199 in 200), multiplied by the chance of stopping there (1 in 200).

i.e. $\frac{199}{200} \times \frac{1}{200} =$ the chance of stopping at the second destination

Similarly for the third destination the chances of obtaining brand X are

$$\frac{199}{200} \times \frac{199}{200} \times \frac{1}{200} = \frac{199^2}{200} \times \frac{1}{200}$$

From the above example it is possible to derive the intervening opportunities model, by assessing the probability that a given trip will stop in a given zone of destination j.

Let L =Probability of a particular trip origin stopping at any randomly chosen destination (i.e. $\frac{1}{200}$ in the above example)

V =Number of destinations found closer to the point of origin i, than zone j

Vj=Number of destinations in zone j

The probability that a given trip will get to j is given by $(1-L)^V$ (i.e. $(1-\frac{1}{200})^2$ in the above example) and the chance that the trip will not find a satisfactory destination in j and go on to the next zone after j is $(1-L)^{V+Vj}$. Therefore the chance that the given trip will have stopped in j is the difference between the two values, i.e. $(1-L)^V-(1-L)^{V+Vj}$.

In practice all the journeys starting from a particular zone will not have the same value for L, i.e. some trips will be more selective than others. To sum the infinitely large number of probabilities, which would vary from point to point, involved the use of calculus, but because of the difficulties associated with this integration the basic model was simplified for practical use to

$$T_{i-j} = \sum_{L^{\min}}^{L^{\max}} T_{i(G)} L\left((1-L)^V-(1-L)^{V+Vj}\right)$$

where T_{i-j}=Number of trips from zone i to j

$T_{i(G)}L$=Total number of trips generated from zone i, with a particular L value

119

$(1-L)^V$=Probability that a given trip will get to a given destination

$(1-L)^{V+V_j}$=Probability that a given trip will not find a satisfactory destination in j and go on to the next zone.

N.B. the term $((1-L)^V-(1-L)^{V+V_j})$=Probability function P_j.

To synthesise existing and future travel patterns using this model it is necessary to provide an operational definition of V, i.e. all trip destinations closer to the zone or origin than the zone j. Distance and cost of travel were considered in Chicago but were eventually rejected because cost is difficult to measure, and distance takes no account of varying travel speeds. Travel time was eventually chosen as the most appropriate method of determining the order of search likely to be adopted in deciding on the destination for a particular journey from a particular zone of origin.

The probability of a particular trip origin stopping at any randomly chosen destination (L) must also be given an operational definition. To reduce the amount of computational work in the Chicago study trip, origins for every zone were classified into long trips and short trips, L_{max} and L_{min}, and the two values for L were determined by fitting empirically values which satisfied for the short trips the observed proportion of journeys taking place within the zone of origin, and for the long trips the observed total of vehicle miles of travel in the system.

Two basic assumptions were essential to fit this model to the existing travel patterns.

1 '... all trips in all zones falling in either one of the two groups could be represented by a single value of L.'

2 '... the larger and more specialised journeys would be restricted so that trips from residential origins could only connect with non-residential destinations, and *vice versa*.'[15]

To utilise the model in the projection of future travel patterns and to derive values for L and V it is necessary to assume that

a the present-day proportion of trips satisfied without leaving their zone of origin will hold good to the design year, and

b the future transportation network of the area under consideration is known.

In Chicago these two assumptions were made, although the future values for L were modified by yet another assumption, that the volume of destinations in each zone would increase thereby producing lower values for L. To simulate the procedure likely to be adopted by a future traveller in choosing his destination it was assumed that the existing comprehensive transport network would be improved rather than materially altered, with the result that the relative closeness of present-day zones would not be altered in the future.

2 *Competing opportunities*: The competing opportunities model, which was developed from an analysis of 1947 origin and destination data, was used to analyse the data collected in the *Penn–Jersey Transportation Study*. The method involves the direct application of probability theory in conjunction with certain aspects of the gravity model and the Fratar technique of successive approximations:

The basic formula is

$$T_{i-j} = T_{i(G)} \times P_j'$$

where T_{i-j} =Number of one way trips from zone i to zone j
$T_{i(G)}$ =Total number of trips originating in zone i
P_j' =adjusted probability of stopping at destination j

The adjusted probability of stopping is defined as the product of two independent probabilities—the probability of attraction and the probability of satisfaction.

The theoretical derivation of this model and its application to trip distribution is fully explained in an article by A. R. Tomazinis,[16] but in outline is as follows.

1 Theoretical derivation—assume a universe with total population N, and two sub-populations H and S. Part of sub-population H forms part of sub-population S which is GHS. The probability of randomly selecting a member of the universe population N, which is also a member of the sub-populations S and H, is determined.

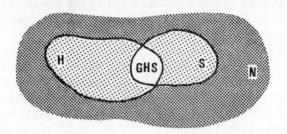

*Fig. 7   Diagrammatic representation of theoretical universe (N) and
sub-population (H and S)—theoretical derivation of intervening
opportunities*

SOURCE   A. R. Tomazinis, A new method of trip distribution in an urban
area, *Highway Research Board, Bulletin No. 347* (1962).

The probability that the chosen member is a member of
sub-population H, $(P_{(H)})$ is

$$P_{(H)} = \frac{H}{N}$$

The probability that it is a member of sub-population S is

$$P_{(S)} = \frac{S}{N}$$

and the probability that it is a member of both H and S is

$$P_{(HS)} = \frac{GHS}{N}$$

To obtain the probability that $P_{(H)}$ will take place given that
$P_{(S)}$ has already taken place, it is necessary to define the
conditional probability of $P_{(H)}$ given $P_{(S)}$, $P_{(H/S)}$: In terms of
formal probability theory this is given by

$$P_{(H/S)} = \frac{P_{(HS)}}{P_{(S)}} = \frac{\dfrac{GHS}{N}}{\dfrac{S}{N}} = \frac{GHS}{S}$$

Application to trip distribution: The study region is divided into a series of 'time districts' each having a certain time distance separating it from the zone of origin. If it is assumed that the population of the universe (N) is the equivalent to the total trip opportunities in the study area; that the number of trip opportunities within one travel time district from one zone of origin is H; and that the total number of trip opportunities within the district of destination is S, then by applying the conditional probability equation already defined, it is possible to determine $P_{(S/H)}$—the probability of attraction.

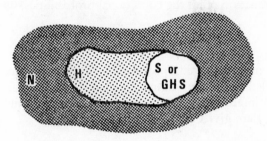

Fig. 8   Diagrammatic representation of study area and travel time districts—application of intervening opportunities to trip distribution

SOURCE   A. R. Tomazinis, A new method of trip distribution in an urban area, *Highway Research Board, Bulletin No. 347* (1962).

Application to trip distribution

$$P_{(H)} = \frac{H}{N}; \quad P_{(S)} = \frac{S}{N}; \quad P_{(SH)} = \frac{S}{N} = P_{(S)}$$

which gives

$$P_{(S/H)} = \frac{P_{(SH)}}{P_{(H)}} = \frac{\dfrac{S}{N}}{\dfrac{H}{N}} = \frac{S}{H}$$

In simple terms this implies that the probability that a trip will go to a district depends on the ratio between the trip opportunities in the district and its competing opportunites.

The total number of trip opportunities in the study area is used indirectly to define the pertinent (adjusted) probability. The summation of the probability of each district within the area should be unity because the total trips distributed should equal the trips available in the district of origin.

Hence $$\sum P'_i = 1$$

Where i represents 1, 2, ... n i.e. all the districts into which trips are distributed.

To obtain $\sum P'_i = 1$, the $P_{(S/H)}$ of each district is divided by the summation of all the conditional probabilities. Thus

$$\frac{P_{i\ (S/H)}}{\sum P_{i(S/H)}} = P'_i$$

The new, adjusted, probability of each district is then multiplied by the trip origins of each district of origin to obtain the trip interchange, e.g. the one-way trips from district x to district y are given by

$$T_{xy} = P'_y \times T_x$$

where P'_y = the adjusted probability of district y
T_x = the trip origins in district x
T_{xy} = one way trips from district x to y

Once the above process has been repeated for each district, and the total number of trips into each district from all other districts estimated, then the use of a balancing technique may be required to bring the estimated and actual trips into equilibrium.

Conclusions

The opportunity methods have been successfully used by three of the most comprehensive transportation studies made to date, and as a result have been thoroughly researched and tested. They are based on a concept which seems logical, i.e. that trips lengthen only because they fail to find an acceptable destination closer to their origin. The formulae evolved are computationally convenient and well behaved mathematically, and there is a possibility that once existing data has been used to calibrate and obtain values for their parameters, and the models shown to be reliable, the future need for comprehensive origin and destination studies will be eliminated.

However, there are certain problems associated with their use. The simplicity of the earlier methods has been lost and the introduction of more complex relationships as a basis for these methods has resulted in the need for more experienced staff and large computer facilities. An iterative process is necessary to ensure that the number of trips arriving at a particular zone of destination agrees with the number of trips established at the trip generation stage. To date, extensive and expensive surveys have been necessary to calibrate these models but the most serious disadvantage associated with their use is that the methods can account only for a relative change in the time-distance relationship between all the zones in a given urban area. Consequently their use like the growth factor methods is restricted to those areas where no major changes in land use or the transportation network are expected.

Evaluation of trip distribution models and future developments

The growth factor methods of trip distribution have been thoroughly used and tested. The advantages and problems associated with their use are well known and have been out-lined already. The synthetic models are still in the process of being developed, tested and compared, and although their individual disadvantages are known their comparative efficiency is still in question. Work by Witheford[17] in connection with the *Pittsburgh Area Transportation Study* led him to the conclusion that the intervening opportunities model was better than the gravity model in simulating trip distribution, because the gravity model required extensive adjustments to achieve adequate results. However, the gravity model tested by him was not stratified by trip purpose, and did not include the socio-economic adjustment factors.

K. E. Heanue and C. E. Pyers[18] on the other hand have tested a stratified gravity model including socio-economic adjustment factors, against the Fratar and opportunity methods and concluded that as a technique it is perfectly adequate in most respects.

More recent work carried out by H. Lanson and J. Dearinger[19] compared and tested four methods of forecasting the zone to zone interchange of industrial work trips. The four models tested included the gravity model, the electrostatic model, the competing opportunities model and the multiple regression model, and the work journey movement was chosen because of its position as the most significant, repetitive and easily forecasted movement.

The basis of the comparison was the existing origin and destination data for the Lexington/Lafayette area of Kentucky, and the predictive accuracies of the four models were evaluated by computing the root-mean-square error (RMS).

The conclusions reached by Lanson and Dearinger were that

1 the multiple regression model gave the most accurate distribution results both numerically and by RMS.

2 the gravity model—which included socio-economic adjustment factors—gave the most accurate distribution pattern by RMS for the theoretical models.

3 the competing opportunities model was the most accurate theoretical model in terms of the total number of trips distributed to a zone, but the patterns of distribution were divergent.

4 the electrostatic model produced varied results overall.

In general terms Lanson and Dearinger concluded that the gravity model when used with only one purpose is simple and easy to use, and is sensitive to changes in travel time. The multiple regression model is flexible in that any variable thought to have an influence on trip distribution can be included. It is easy to understand and can be applied to any urban area for any trip purpose. The electrostatic model is relatively inexpensive to apply as it operates independently of existing movement patterns, whilst the competing opportunities model requires less origin and destination data for calibration than the gravity model. In terms of accuracy, however, the multiple linear regression and the gravity models are favoured by Lanson and Dearinger.

Future development

Of the trip distribution models discussed the gravity, opportunity and multiple regression models show the greatest promise for future development. The growth factor methods, although simple to apply and useful in stable conditions, have little relevance in a situation which is changing rapidly. The development of a 'purpose' Fratar method offset some of the limitations associated with growth factors, but the problem of zero flows in the base year remains.

The gravity model, although well documented and tested, could be improved by developing more sophisticated attraction and resistance parameters for use in the formulae. Attraction parameters based as they now are on a single factor such as zonal employment, or population, could well be developed so that one factor is produced combining aspects of all these single factors. Similarly, a more sophisticated resistance parameter could be developed combining the effect of distance, time, and cost, whilst the relationship between socio-economic variables and the K–adjustment factor needs further examination.

The opportunity methods have two major disadvantages which must be overcome before they can be considered universally applicable.

1 The 'L' values, as determined for the Chicago study, change with time, and to overcome this difficulty research is needed into trip length trends.

2 The methods cannot easily account for an absolute change which might take place to alter the 'separation' between a given pair of zones, e.g. the construction of a bridge such as the Severn or Forth road-bridges would make it extremely difficult for an opportunity model developed before the opening of these bridges to be used to distribute movements for a design year after their opening. Again further research is needed to overcome this difficulty.

The multiple regression model would appear to have the advantage over the other methods described. It is extremely flexible in that any variable thought to have an influence on travel patterns can be included in the basic equation. However, there is a danger that although a satisfactory relationship between independent variables can be derived for the present movement patterns, the variables represented in the equation may not all be 'explanatory' variables, with the result that the projection of non-explanatory variables to the base year could produce erroneous trip distribution patterns. Research is therefore necessary to derive a more satisfactory understanding of the motivations giving rise to movements before the multiple regression model can be used with confidence. In addition, the application of a separate equation to each pair of zones in the study area involves an enormous amount of data collecton and computational procedures. The work carried out by F. R. Wilson in his analysis of journey to work movements[20] indicates that some of this time-consuming basic work can be eliminated by stratifying zones, but again more work on these matters is required.

Should all the above problems associated with trip distribution be eliminated by further research, then great improvements in the overall accuracy of this part of the transportation planning process would be achieved. Whether these improvements would transform the whole process from a highly suspect estimating procedure to a precise working tool is another matter.

References

1 Davinroy T. R., Ridley T. M., Wootton H. J., Predicting future travel, *Traffic Engineering and Control* (1963).
2 Oi W. Y. and Schuldiner P. W., *An Analysis of Urban Travel Demands*, North-Western University Press, Chicago (1962).
3 Pollard Jr. W. S., Forecasting traffic with a modified growth factor procedure, *Highway Research Board*, Bulletin No. 297 (1961).
4 Pollard Jr. W. S., *op. cit.*
5 Fratar T. J., Vehicle trip distribution by successive approximations, *Traffic Quarterly*, Eno Foundation (1954).
6 Bevis H., Forecasting zonal traffic volumes, *Traffic Quarterly*, Eno Foundation (1956).
7 Reilly W. J., *The Law of Retail Gravitation* (2nd edition), Pilbury, New York (1953).
8 Casey Jr. H. J., Applications to traffic engineering of the law

of retail gravitation, *Traffic Quarterly*, Eno Foundation (1955).

9 Calibrating and testing a gravity model for any size urban area, *U.S Department of Commerce, Bureau of Public Roads*, Washington (1965).

10 Howe R. T., A theoretical prediction of work trip patterns in the Minneapolis-St. Paul area, *Highway Research Board, Bulletin No. 347* (1962).
See also: Howe R. T., A theoretical prediction of work trip patterns. *Highway Research Board*, Bulletin No. 253 (1960).

11 Osofsky S., A multiple regression approach to forecasting urban area traffic volumes, *Proceedings of the American Association of State Highway Officials*, Washington (1958).

12 Chicago Area Transportation Study, Final Report Volume II (1960).

13 Stouffer S. A., Intervening opportunities: a theory relating to mobility and distance, *American Sociology Review*, 4 (1940).

14 Chicago Area Transportation Study, *op. cit.*

15 Chicago Area Transportation Study, *op cit.*

16 Tomazinis A. R., A new method of trip distribution in an urban area, *Highway Research Board*, Bulletin No. 347 (1962).

17 Witheford D. K., A comparison of trip distribution by opportunity model and gravity model, *Pittsburgh Area Transportation Study* (1961).

18 Heanue K. E. and Pyers C. E., A comparative evaluation of trip distribution procedures, *Highway Research Board*, Record No. 114 (1966).

19 Lanson H. and Dearinger J., A comparison of four work journey distribution models, *Proceedings of the American Society of Civil Engineers*, Highway Division, Volume 93, No. H.W. 2 (1967).

20 Wilson F. R., *The Journey to Work—Modal Split*, Maclaren (1967).

5 Traffic assignment

Introduction

Traffic assignment is the process of allocating a given set of trip interchanges to a specific transportation system. It can be used to estimate the volume of traffic on various links of the system for any future year, or to simulate present conditions. The traffic assignment process requires as input a complete description of either the proposed or existing transportation system, and a matrix of interzonal trip movements. The output of the process is an estimate of the traffic volumes on each link of the transportation system, although the more sophisticated assignment techniques also include directional turning movements at intersections.

The purposes of traffic assignment are, broadly:

1 To assess the deficiencies in the existing transportation system by assigning estimated future trips to the existing system.

2 To evaluate the effects of limited improvements and extensions to the existing transportation system by assigning estimated future trips to the network which includes these improvements.

3 To develop construction priorities by assigning estimated future trips for intermediate years to the transportation system proposed for those years.

4 To test alternative transportation system proposals by systematic and readily repeatable procedures.

5 To provide design hour volumes and turning movements. Broadly speaking three major alternative procedures have been developed to assign estimated future trips to a transportation system. They are

 a All or nothing assignments
 b Diversion curve assignments
 c Capacity restraint assignments

The choice of assignment procedure to be adopted in any particular transportation study depends largely on the purpose of that study, and the degree of sophistication required in the output.

Assignment techniques have developed in conjunction with origin and destination studies, to determine the route likely to be taken by interzonal trips traditionally illustrated by some form of desire line diagram. In the early 1950s considerable difficulty was experienced in assessing the driver's choice of route to complete his interzonal trip, and route choice decisions were often arbitrarily based on personal knowledge and an assessment of travel time, distance and user cost.

Empirical studies were undertaken in the United States, in an attempt to relate choice of route to time and distance factors, and as a result the American Association of State Highway Officials developed a standard traffic diversion curve as recommended policy for determining the future use of urban highways. However, this technique was only capable of dealing with a single motorway with existing parallel routes.

In 1957 a major breakthrough in traffic assignment occurred. The Armour Research Foundation working on the problem of traffic assignment in the *Chicago Area Transportation Study* developed a computer programme capable of finding the minimum time or distance path through a network. This programme was only capable of handling a very small network, but provided a basis for further research, which resulted in the development of a programme for a large high-speed computer capable of assigning traffic to the existing and proposed street system for the entire Chicago area. Today this 'minimum path' technique of assignment is known as the 'all or nothing' assignment procedure.

Further research led, in 1960, to the development by the

General Electric Computer Department in co-operation with the District of Columbia, of an assignment programme capable of prohibiting selected turns in the calculation of the minimum path. This latest modification has been developed into the capacity restraining technique of traffic assignment.

General procedure

The traffic assignment procedure is based on the selection of a minimum time path over an actual route between zones. Although the process is invariably carried out by computer it can be done manually. For the task to be accomplished by computer it is necessary to describe the highway network code and store it in the computer's memory. The computer then chooses the minimum path between zones, assigns estimated trips to this path and accumulates traffic volumes for each section of the route.

For coding purposes the highway network is broken down into links and nodes. A link is defined as the one-way part of the route between two intersections and, depending on the assignment technique to be used, detailed information concerning the length, speed and/or travel time of vehicles, capacity and existing volumes on each link is coded and stored in the computer. Nodes are of two types—zone centroid, and intersection nodes where two or more links meet. Nodes are identified by a numeric code which is applied systematically whilst links are identified by the node number at each end of the link.

Once the coding is completed the data is punched, checked and stored in the computer, which then chooses the minimum time path between zones after a systematic search and accumulation of travel times stored in the memory.

The minimum time path is the shortest route from one zone centroid to another, and this route is known as a 'tree'. It is selected after the computer, moving outwards from the starting node, has compared travel times between adjacent nodes to derive the quickest path between all nodes. At each node in the network the travel time back to the starting centroid and the immediate previous node are recorded syste-

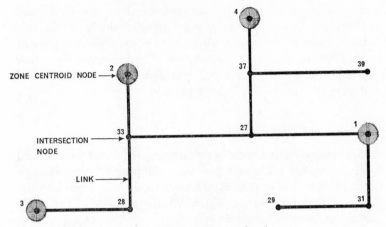

Fig. 9   Highway network description—links and nodes

matically to derive the travel time and route between the starting node and all other nodes.

The next stage in the process is to assign the zone to zone trips to the links on the minimum path routes (or trees) between the various zones. Trips generated by each zone are dealt with successively, and the process is repeated until all trips from all centroids have been loaded on to the links of the network.

At this stage traffic loads on individual links of the network may be in excess of the capacity of the proposed facilities, and a new set of minimum time paths between zones must be derived, using a set of adjusted travel times. If this is done automatically the programme is known as a capacity restraint programme, and adjustments are made to the network after the computer has checked the ratio of the assigned traffic volume to the capacity for each link, and in accordance with a predetermined relationship. This relationship is based on the assumption that as the volume of traffic on a link increases so the travel time on that link increases. Thus the speed necessary to travel that link is reduced just as increased congestion causes speeds to be lowered in real situations.

Traffic assignments can be produced for total daily traffic, or any subdivision of the 24-hour period, such as the morning or evening peak periods; for directional or non-directional flows; and for any particular purpose or mode. However, it is more usual to first make an average daily traffic assignment (ADT) and from this obtain traffic assignments for other periods of the day by using conversion factors determined during the survey stage of the process.

Number and types of assignment

Generally speaking three basic categories of assignment should be undertaken in the transportation planning process although the number and type of assignments made will depend on the size of the area under examination, the purpose of the study and the financial resources available.

1 The assignment of existing trips to the existing network to check the adequacy of the assignment procedure by testing its ability mechanically to reproduce the existing travel patterns.

2 The assignment of estimated future trips to the existing network plus the committed extensions and improvements. This type of assignment is undertaken to determine the deficiencies in the existing network and to provide a framework for the development of further additions and improvements to this network.

3 The assignment of estimated future trips to the future network. At this stage the effect of land-use distribution and the proposed transportation system must be carefully analysed and it is usual practice to assign the estimated future trips to several alternative land-use plans with their accompanying transport systems.

Optimum programming of the network construction can be determined by partial network assignments, whilst assignments made by five yearly incremental periods will allow the evaluation of the procedures adopted and provide for future adjustments in forecasting and assignment, if necessary, instead of waiting for the forecast year to arrive.

Diversion curves in traffic assignment

For any trip from one zone to another there are usually several alternative routes, which can be chosen by the person making the trip. Each route has its own 'travel resistance' derived from its characteristics of distance, travel time, speed and level of service. These characteristics are evaluated either consciously or subconsciously by the driver before a particular route is chosen. Thus a route with a high travel resistance, e.g. a busy urban street with bus stops, parked cars, numerous inter-sections, and pedestrians will not be used by as many drivers as a comparable route with low travel resistance. This concept of travel resistance is used in traffic assignment by deriving a quantified measure of the resistance and examining empirically the relationship between this measure and the usage of two alternative routes. Diversion curves are then derived from these empirical studies to show what proportion of drivers are likely to transfer to a new urban motorway, should one be constructed.

Numerous diversion curves have been constructed using different measures of travel resistance, the principal ones are:
Travel time saved—(derived from A–B);
Distance saved (C–D), Travel-time ratio (B/A); Distance ratio (D/C);
Cost ratio (F/E); Travel time/Distance saved (known as Californian curves) and Distance/Speed ratio (known as Detroit curves), where
A = Travel time via quickest non-motorway route
B = Travel time via motorway
C = Distance via shortest non-motorway route
D = Distance via motorway
E = Cost on alternative non-motorway route
F = Cost on motorway

Three diversion curves are in current use today—the time ratio curve, the travel time and distance saved curve, and the distance speed ratio curve.

Of the remaining curves the travel time saved diversion curve tends to separate trips by length, as the longer trips usually have a large travel time saving.

The distance saved diversion curve is sensitive to small changes in distance, and because distance alone cannot account for as many 'travel resistance' factors as travel time does these curves are generally unreliable and are infrequently used today.

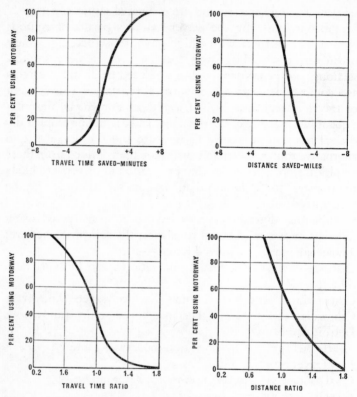

Fig. 10   *Typical diversion curves (based on North American data)*

The distance ratio diversion curve is again based on an inadequate measure of travel resistance and has the added disadvantage that for trips with the same distance ratio, the same diversion curve is used, regardless of trip length.

The cost ratio diversion curve is not used extensively, mainly because of the problems associated with placing a money value on time.

Travel time ratio curve

The travel time ratio curve bases the percentage of trips to be assigned to a motorway or new facility on the ratio of the travel time via the motorway to the travel time via the quickest alternate route. The curve is an *S*-shaped curve, and using the Bureau of Public Roads curve as an example it is seen that the percentage of trips using the motorway varies from 100% at a time ratio of 0·5 or less, to zero% at a time ratio of 1·5 or more. If travel time by both the motorway and the alternative route is equal, then 42% (approximately) of the trips are assigned to the motorway, because such trips with their faster speeds require a larger travel distance.

One difficulty associated with the use of the travel time ratio curve is that, regardless of length, trips with the same travel time ratio are given the same diversion rate.

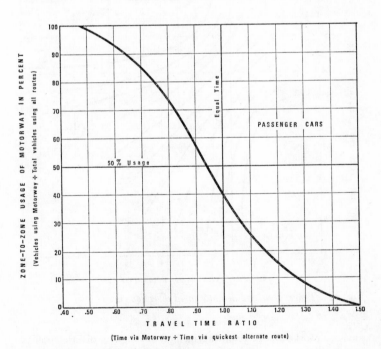

Fig. 11   Bureau of Public Roads diversion curves

137

Travel time and distance saved diversion curves

This set of diversion curves, developed by the California Division of Highways,[1] consists of a family of hyperbolas, constructed on a mathematical basis, using the results of observations on freeways in California. The assumptions basic to the derivation of these curves were

1 Factors other than time and distance cannot be measured explicitly, nor forecasted, and can therefore be ignored.

2 The greater the travel time and distance saved the greater the usage.

3 When only small savings in time and distance occur some drivers will transfer to the motorway, others will not.

4 Some drivers will drive any distance to save travel time; few

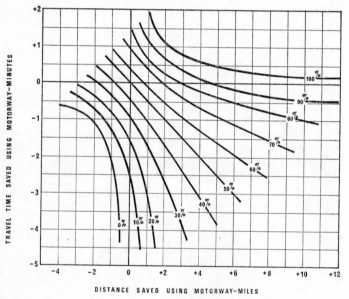

Fig. 12   Travel time and distance saved diversion curve

SOURCE   Moskowitz K. California method of assigning diverted traffic to proposed freeways. *Highways Research Board, Bulletin No. 130* (1956).

drivers will select the shortest route in terms of distance at the expense of travel time.

These curves are expressed in the equation

$$P = 50 + 50(d + \tfrac{1}{2}t) \; [(d - \tfrac{1}{2}t)^2 + 4 \cdot 5] - \tfrac{1}{2}$$

where P = Percentage of motorway usage
d = distance saved in miles via the motorway
t = time saved in minutes via the motorway

Speed distance ratio curves

This family of curves, developed for the Detroit Area Traffic Study,[2] relates the percentage of motorway use to speed and distance ratios, using the assumption that although time, distance and speed are the principal factors affecting a driver's choice of route, because they are interrelated it is only necessary to define two of them.

Distance ratio and speed ratio were adopted with the result that if this set of curves is used, then the need for a travel time study is eliminated as a ratio between speeds on a motorway or new route and on existing city streets can be assumed.

The speed ratio used in this method is the average trip speed via the new route divided by the average trip speed on the existing city street route.

It can be seen from Figure 13 that with a speed ratio of 1 and a distance ratio of 1, approximately 45% of the trips are assigned to the new route.

Diversion curves are constructed to enable assignments to be made to proposed transport facilities. However, they have their limitations. Although present-day travel resistance characteristics are reflected in the curves themselves, the extent to which these will remain constant in the future depends on the extent and nature of proposed changes in the transport system. For example, if the highway network is completely changed and the level of service improved the characteristics of the old network are also likely to change. At the same time the attitude of drivers towards factors such as time, distance, comfort and convenience can also change. In general terms diversion curve assignments are not ideally suited to large area transportation

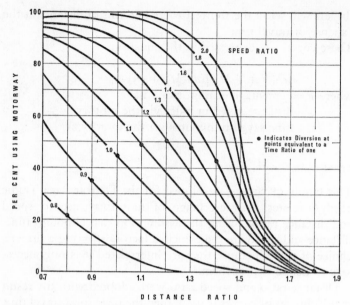

Fig. 13 Distance and speed ratio diversion curve

SOURCE *Detroit Metropolitan Area Traffic Study* (1956).

studies where far-reaching changes are proposed for the transport system. However, for small towns where minor extensions and improvements are contemplated they can be used effectively and economically.

All or nothing assignments

All or nothing assignments are based on the assumption that the path taken by vehicles travelling from zone of origin to zone of destination will be the one with least travel resistance. Although travel resistance can be measured in terms of distance, cost, time, or some combination of these factors, the measure normally used is that of time.

The basic procedure in all or nothing assignments involves:
1 The description and coding of the network into links and nodes.

140

2 The determination of minimum path time from each zone with originating traffic to all other zones. (This stage is often referred to as 'build trees'.)

3 The assignment of all traffic flows from each zone to every other zone by the appropriate minimum path, and the aggregation of total flows on each link in the defined network.

Description and Coding of network: This process is similar for all traffic assignment techniques and has been outlined in the introduction.

Determination of minimum paths: If done manually the determination of minimum paths between zone centroids is a laborious and time-consuming task, as the following example illustrates.

The object of this example is to determine the minimum path from Zone Centroid 1 to all other nodes on the network.

1 Start at Zone Centroid 1 and proceed outwards to all connecting nodes. At each node record the travel time to it.

In this example

From Node 1 to Node 16 $(T_{16})=2\cdot0$ minutes.

From Node 1 to Node 22 $(T_{22})=3\cdot0$ minutes.

2 The Node closest to Zone Centroid 1 is considered next, i.e., 16, thus

From Node 16 to Node 15 $=3\cdot0$ minutes

$\therefore$ From Node 1–16–15 $(T_{15})=5\cdot0$ minutes

From Node 16 to Node 17 $=3\cdot0$ minutes

$\therefore$ From Node 1–16–17 $(T_{17})=5\cdot0$ minutes

3 The next closest node to Zone Centroid 1 is then considered, i.e. Node 22. Thus

From Node 22–13 $=3\cdot0$ minutes

$\therefore$ From Node 1–22–13 $(T_{13})=6\cdot0$ minutes

From Node 22–17 $=3\cdot0$ minutes

$\therefore$ From Node 1–22–17 $(T_{17})=6\cdot0$ minutes

At this stage there are two routes from Node 1–17 (i.e. 1–16–17 and 1–22–17) taking 5 and 6 minutes respectively. As the assignment technique requires that only the shortest route is used, the longer route 1–22–17 of 6 minutes is eliminated.

4 This process is repeated until all nodes have been reached

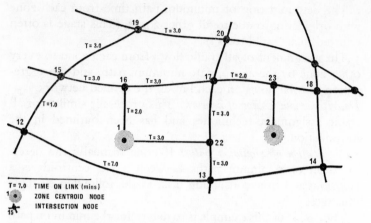

Fig. 14   Network for calculation of minimum path

via the minimum time path from Zone Centroid 1. The same procedure is used to 'build trees' for all the zones in the network. Fortunately it is possible to build minimum path trees by using a computer to select the minimum path on the basis of the information concerning journey time or other travel resistance factors that have been fed into it.

Assignment

All traffic flows from zone centroids to all other zone centroids are now assigned to the minimum path trees already calculated. A simple example illustrates the procedure adopted, which can be carried out manually or by computer.

In Figure 15 only the minimum paths from Zone Centroid 1 to Nodes 2, 3 and 4 are given. The minimum paths in the reverse direction from Nodes 2, 3 and 4 to Node 1 may well be different, as the links may not have the same travel time in the reverse direction.

Assume that for the above example the traffic flows to be assigned from Home Node 1 are 1–2   2,400 vehicles

                                     1–3   1,726 vehicles

                                       1–4   3,172 vehicles

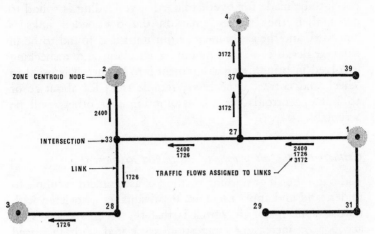

Fig. 15   Minimum path tree calculated from Node 1 in sample network

The minimum path from 1–2 is 1–27–33–2 and consequently 2,400 vehicles are assigned to each link of the network between 1 and 2. Similarly, the minimum paths between 1–3 and 1–4 are 1–27–33–28–3 and 1–27–37–4 respectively, and the appropriate vehicles are assigned to each link.

This process is repeated for each zone in relation to every other zone and the total number of vehicles on each link of the network is then aggregated.

In the limited example above it can be seen that link 1–27 carries 7,298 vehicles, link 27–33 4,126 vehicles, link 27–37 3,172 vehicles, and so on.

In addition to the traffic volumes on each link of the network, the turning movements at each junction are also derived through the same procedure.

To complete this stage of the process a check must be carried out to ensure that no link in the network has been overloaded. (An overloaded link is one on which the total of the trips assigned to it is in excess of the capacity of that link.) If the assignment has been carried out by computer then a tabulation is printed-out giving the traffic flows on all the links in the route of minimum time paths thus enabling a manual check to be made for overloading. If overloading is found to occur then the journey time on the overloaded links is amended, and the assignment re-run until it is found to be in balance. Because of the amount of checking and rechecking involved in bringing an assignment into balance it is usual to 'check and correct if necessary sample trees for about 20 or 30 home centroids on the assumption that others will be acceptable'.[3]

Criticisms of the 'all or nothing' assignment technique

Although the all or nothing method of assignment is simple to understand and apply there are disadvantages associated with its use. One major drawback is that the technique takes no account of increasing congestion associated with increased volumes and assigns too many vehicles to the better routes as travel time on these routes will be better than on the multi-purpose streets. In real-life situations, however, it has been found that vehicle drivers use both routes. Another problem arises from the fact that for longer journeys in terms of distance more people tend to transfer to motorways yet the all or nothing assignment technique based on shortest journey times ignores this factor.

Small differences in journey times by different routes between the same origin and destination can bring about unrealistic journey paths when the all or nothing assignment is used. Indeed Buchanan and Partners found that in the all or nothing assignment procedure used to support the development of the inner relief road across Christchurch Meadow, Oxford, 'the differences (in journey time) are so small that drivers could hardly be expected to be aware of them'.[4]

Capacity restraint assignment[5]

A capacity restraint assignment is an alternative method of dealing with overloaded links in the network. It is carried out entirely by the computer and is completely automatic. The input required by capacity restraint assignments is similar in many ways to that required by 'all or nothing' assignments. In addition the practical capacity of each link of the network is fed into the computer as well as journey time. The first stage of the capacity restraint assignment involves the building of minimum path trees in exactly the same way as they are built for the all or nothing technique. Traffic is then assigned to these minimum paths but as the assigned volume on each link approaches the practical capacity the computer, through an iterative procedure in which loaded link information is used as a feedback to the tree-building process, automatically lowers the assumed speeds on the affected links thereby making these links less attractive to traffic.

The procedure for the description and coding of the network required for the capacity restraint assignment is identical to that carried out for the all or nothing technique.

The first set of minimum paths between zone centroids is also determined in a similar manner, using the practical capacity of each link and the speed at which traffic would flow on each link when loaded to capacity. Traffic from each zone of origin to each zone of destination is then assigned to the network and the loads on each link are compared with the practical capacity of that link. If a link is found to be overloaded then a new journey time which makes allowance for the effect of congestion or excessive traffic flows on speed, is calculated for that link. It is assumed that the relationship between journey time (or speed) and volume on each link in a highway network can be expressed by the equation:[5]

$$T = T_0 \left[1 + 0.15 \left(\frac{\text{Assigned volume}}{\text{Practical capacity}} \right)^4 \right]$$

where

T = Journey time at which assigned volume can travel on the appropriate link

T_0 = Base journey time at zero volume which = journey time at practical capacity $\times 0.87$

Using this equation it is possible to determine the speed at which the assigned volume could theoretically be carried. e.g. Assume that a link 27–32 is one mile long, and has a practical capacity of 40,000 vehicles per day, and a speed at that capacity of 40 m.p.h. The travel time on that link is therefore $1\frac{1}{2}$ minutes. Travel time at zero volume (T_0) is $1 \cdot 5 \times 0 \cdot 87$ minutes $= 1 \cdot 31$ minutes. After the network has been loaded it is found that link 27–32 has 60,000 vehicles per day assigned to it. Using the above formula, the travel time for the assigned volume is estimated.

$$T = 1 \cdot 31 \left[1 + 0 \cdot 15 \left(\frac{60,000}{40,000} \right)^4 \right]$$

$$1 \cdot 31 [1 + \cdot 76]$$

2·3 minutes (or 26 m.p.h. at which 60,000 vehicles per day can travel on link 27–32).

The new speed, based on an adjustment of the balance travel time is used in the next iteration to minimise the imbalance of volume on the link. However, experience has shown that by changing the travel time on a link an inverse change in the loading occurs. Consequently the full effect of this change is moderated by using a speed for the next iteration which is only one quarter of the way from the last assignment speed to the new balance speed. Thus in the above example a speed of 40 m.p.h. corresponds to a travel time 1·5 minutes, whilst the travel time at the first assigned volume is 2·3 minutes. To find the speed to use in the next iteration one quarter of the difference between 2·3 and 1·5 minutes (or 0·8 minutes) is added to the previous travel time. This results in a value of 1·7 minutes or a speed of 35 m.p.h.

It has been found that this method of adjustment eliminates large oscillations of loads on the links from one iteration to the next. The next step in the procedure involves the building of a new set of trees by using the adjusted speeds on each link. Traffic is assigned to the modified network; the volume to capacity ratio is examined again and if necessary further adjustments are made to overloaded links. The process is continued for as many iterations as desired although experience has shown that after four iterations the accuracy of the assignments does not improve appreciably.

Alternative improved method of assignment[6]

Recent work carried out by the Traffic Branch of the Department of Highways and Transportation of the Greater London Council has shown that capacity restraint assignments tend to produce unrealistic results by assigning local traffic movements to the primary road network rather than to equally convenient secondary routes. In theory this problem can be overcome by a 100% inspection and subsequent modification of the trip paths, between pairs of traffic zones. However, such a solution is time-consuming and because of the shunting around of overloads by the capacity restraint programme, well-nigh impossible.

In an attempt to overcome this problem the G.L.C. have strengthened the assignment procedure by interrupting the computer assignment programme at certain stages and substituting manual techniques which enable a comprehensive check of all minimum time paths to be made, and to control the type of trips to be assigned to the Primary Network.

Basically, the new improved alternative assignment procedure rests on the assumption that only the longer distance trips will use the primary network. Trips between adjacent zones will generally use the existing secondary network.

Check on minimum time paths

Using the assumption that only longer distance trips will use the primary network it is argued that the path taken between one group of zones to another group of zones some distance apart will for much of the distance follow a common route, diverging only at the beginning and end of the journey.

Therefore after the first assignment of the longer distance trips has been carried out, a visual inspection of the middle distance part of the route between groups of zones is all that is necessary. If this is satisfactory, then the inspection is extended to those routes linking zone centroids to the start and end of the middle distance part of the route. Using this concept of the middle distance, a comprehensive inspection of all minimum paths can be carried out quite rapidly.

Control of trips using primary network

To ensure that the assignment procedure only assigns the longer distance movements to the primary network, the origin and destination trip matrix is inspected visually. Using predetermined criteria about the constitution of long distance trips, a Trip Classification Table is produced, differentiating between long and short distance trips. The short distance trips are then cancelled from the matrix, and the computer programme assigns the primary trips to the network. After the first assignment the link loadings are checked manually for overloadings and/or underloadings, and the Trip Classification Table reassessed. To cope with overloadings the more local trips between pairs of zones which were previously assigned to the primary network are cancelled, or transferred to another route if a suitable alternative exists. Any spare capacity on the primary network revealed by underloadings and which might reasonably be used by local trips is taken up by reclassifying such trips as primary. Successive iterations are carried out until the primary network is in balance. Secondary (local) trips must be assigned to the secondary network, and this can be accomplished manually. The secondary network must be capable of carrying the secondary load, in addition to the primary trips assigned to the primary network and which have trip ends in the area under consideration. If there are excessive loadings on the secondary network then theoretically additional links are necessary on the primary and/or secondary networks. If for environmental or financial reasons this is not possible, then some restraining influence must be incorporated into the procedure to select primary or secondary trips.

It is possible that in the future these manual techniques can be built into the computer programme, so that the improved alternative assignment procedure can be completed in one pass of the computer.

Assignment to public transport systems

The basic principles of road traffic assignment are directly applicable to the assignment of movements by public transport

148

systems—the concept of travel resistance still holds good. Indeed in most cases the same basic road traffic assignments are used to assign public transport movements, although additional artificial links have to be inserted into the network to take account of factors such as the time taken to transfer from one type of public transport to another, e.g. change from tube to railway, or from car to public transport; and waiting and walking time at origin and destination.

References

1 Moskowitz K., California: method of assigning diverted traffic to proposed freeways, *Highway Research Board*, Bulletin No. 130 (1965).
2 *Detroit Metropolitan Area Traffic Study*, Part II. Future traffic and Long Range Expressway Plan (1956).
3 Reid A. U. and Cottee J. G., *A procedure for the design of a road network*, Report HT/T.1, Greater London Council (1967).
4 Buchanan C. D., Unpublished proof of evidence at Public Enquiry for Oxford Development Plan, Quinquennial Review (1965).
5 Traffic Assignment Manual, *U.S. Department of Commerce, Bureau of Public Roads*, Washington (1964).
6 Reid A. U. and Cottee J. G., *op. cit.*

6 Modal split

Introduction

Modal split can be defined as the proportionate division of the total number of person trips between different methods or modes of travel. It can be expressed numerically as a fraction, ratio or percentage of the total number of trips.

Many different procedures have been developed to derive this split in the transportation planning process, all based on the assumption that of a given total travel demand the proportion carried by bus, tube, surface railway or private motorcar will depend on the standing of each mode of transport in relation to its competitors. The measure of competitiveness is usually derived from an analysis of three sets of factors:

1 characteristics of the journey to be made, e.g. length, time of day the journey is made, purpose of the journey.
2 characteristics of the person making the journey, e.g. car ownership, income, social standing.
3 characteristics of the transportation system, e.g. travel time involved, cost, accessibility, comfort.

Modal split models can be classified into two broad categories:
1 models which are applied prior to the trip distribution stage of the process, and allocate a portion of the total travel demand to the different modes available. These are known as trip end modal split models.
2 models which allocate portions of given trip movements

resulting from trip distribution to the competing modes of transport. These are often referred to as trip interchange modal split models.

Early trip end models utilised only characteristics of the journey to be made and the person making the journey in assessing modal split, e.g. that used in the *Chicago Area Transportation Study*.[1] More recently, however, trip end modal split models have been derived which combine the characteristics of the journey, the person making the journey and the transportation system, e.g. *Southeastern Wisconsin Regional Land Use—Transportation Study*.[2]

The earliest and simplest form of trip interchange modal split model is probably the public transport diversion curve, which attempted to relate the use of public transport to some measure of the relative travel times by competing modes.

However, a fundamental drawback with the simple diversion curve is that it ignores completely the characteristics of the person making the journey, and is incapable of dealing with a complete transportation system at one time. More recently the diversion curve approach to modal split has been refined to take account of journey purpose, time of day, relative travel time and cost, relative travel service and the economic status of the person making the journey, e.g. National Capital Transportation Agency, Washington.[3]

Factors influencing modal choice

The choice of a particular mode of travel in urban areas is neither a static nor a random process. It is influenced either singly or collectively by many factors such as speed, journey length, comfort, convenience, cost, reliability of alternative modes, the availability of specific travel modes, town size, age, and composition; and the socio-economic status of the persons making the journeys.[4] Of all these potential factors influencing modal choice many are incapable of being quantified accurately and reliably. Consequently such factors tend to be omitted or discarded from analyses of modal split on the grounds that their influence is minimal, or can be represented by some other more easily quantified variable. However, these variables which appear to be most significant have been examined in some depth and attempts have been made to derive a reliable measure of their effect on the choice of mode.

Characteristics of the journey

The two most significant factors in this category are journey length and journey purpose.

1 *Journey length:* The length of a journey has been found to influence the modal choice of those persons making that journey.[5] It can be measured in a variety of ways. The airline distance in miles between zone centroids is possibly the simplest measure of journey length. A more accurate measure of distance can be derived from measuring the route distance most likely to be taken between zone centroids, for both public and private means of transport. The time taken to complete a door-to-door journey is another measure of journey length and is often preferred to the measure of distance because it can incorporate the excess travel time associated with journeys.*

The travel time ratio between competing modes (i.e. the relative travel time by public transport compared with the time for the same journey by private motor vehicle) can be used as a measure of journey length. However, its use in isolation can obscure large absolute differences in journey time by competing modes and must be used with caution, or in conjunction with some other measure of distance, e.g. if the travel-time ratio for a journey by private car and public transport is 0·5 and the respective average speeds are 20 m.p.h. and 10 m.p.h., then for a 1-mile journey the time difference between modes is small (3 minutes). But for a 5-mile journey the time difference is 15 minutes, which could well have a greater relative effect on choice of mode than 3 minutes. Thus fewer people can be expected to use public transport as the length of journey increases.

2 *Journey purpose*: Experience has shown that there is a relation-

* Excess travel time is the time spent on that part of a journey which does not involve the use of a vehicle, and includes time spent walking to or from a vehicle, waiting for a vehicle and changing from one vehicle to another.

ship between the numbers using public transport and the purpose of the journey being undertaken. Home-based journeys generally give rise to more public transport journeys than non-home-based journeys, whilst home-based school and work journeys have a higher rate of public transport usage than home-based shopping journeys. This can be explained by the fact that the motor vehicle is essential for some journeys, whilst for others there is open choice.

Characteristics of the traveller

The most significant factors in this category which affect modal split are concerned with the socio-economic characteristics of the households making the journeys and include variables such as income, car ownership, family size and structure, density of residential development, the type of job undertaken, and the location of workplace. Although these factors can be discussed in isolation, in practice they are highly interrelated in the influence they have on modal choice.

1 *Income:* The use of a motor car for any journey depends on one's ability to purchase and maintain it. Car ownership is therefore a function of income—and income must therefore influence modal choice. Figure 16 illustrates a typical relationship between income and public transport usage. Indeed, F. R. Wilson in his work[6] in the Coventry area found that in the area under survey virtually no one with an annual salary in excess of £1,500 p.a. used the Corporation bus system for the work trip.

Various measures of income can be used, e.g. income of head of household, total family income. However, it is often difficult, if not impossible, to derive at a zonal level reliable statistics concerning income for use in such a way. As a substitute other factors such as car ownership, density of residential development, or type of dwelling are used as 'indicators' of income.

2 *Car Ownership:* Car ownership, or the availability of a car, is possibly the most significant factor affecting modal choice. Households without a motorcar have a much lower over-all trip generation rate than car-owning households, and in urban

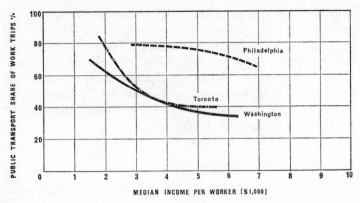

Fig. 16 *Income diversion curve for work trips in peak periods*

SOURCE Hill D. M., Von Cube H. C., Development of a model for fore-casting travel mode choice in urban areas. *Highway Research Board, Record No. 38* (1963).

areas of all sizes, have the heaviest demand for public transport journeys, as a result of having no other available mode of transport.

In contrast with income, it is considered that it is easier to make reliable estimates of future car ownership at a zonal level than to attempt to predict income for the same future date at the same level. Although multi-car ownership substantially increases the total trips performed by members of households, it only marginally reduces the number of journeys made by public transport in the largest urban areas.

3 *Density of residential development:* It has been found that as net residential density decreases, so the use made of public transport decreases. The *Pittsburgh Area Transportation Study*[7] (1958) found that school journeys by public transport are inversely related to net residential density, whilst other journeys by public transport are directly related to it. The inverse relationship between school journeys by public transport and net residential density was attributed to the greater numbers walking to school in the more densely developed areas.

This relationship can be explained by the fact that it is difficult to provide an adequate and economic public transport

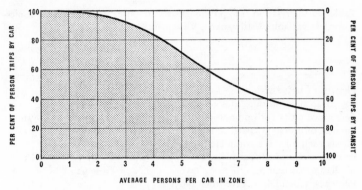

Fig. 17   Effect of car ownership on travel mode

SOURCE   Wilbur Smith and Associates, *Transportation and Parking for Tomorrow's Cities*, New Haven, Connecticut (1966).

service for low density areas. In addition, low density areas tend to be occupied by the middle and higher income groups with the result that levels of car ownership are higher, and consequently the demand for public transport lower.

Conversely, high density areas can be economically and adequately served by public transport. Indeed, such areas usually developed in conjunction with the public transport system and are oriented towards the use of that system. In addition, today lower income residents tend to occupy the high density residential areas vacated by the higher economic classes of a previous age. Thus car ownership tends to be lower in high density areas.

4 *Other socio-economic factors:* Family size, the age–sex structure of the family, the proportion of married females in the labour force, the type of property occupied and the type of employment of the head of household are all factors influencing modal choice.

The table overleaf indicates in general terms the relationship between certain socio-economic variables and the use of public transport, and it is apparent that indicators of high socio-economic status are negatively associated with public transport use.

Table 2. Correlation of public transport—use with selected socio-economic variables (Milwaukee, Wisconsin).

Item	Correlation Coefficient Negative	Correlation Coefficient Positive
Percent of units with two or more automobiles	—·74	
Percent of units with no automobiles		0·71
Percent of units—owner-occupied	—·66	
Median school years completed	—·65	
Percent of divorced females		0·63
Median gross rent	—·62	
Percent civilian labor force unemployed		0·60
Median value of each dwelling unit	—·58	
Median income of families	—·55	
Percent married women, husband present in labor force	—·55	
Percent housing units deteriorated and dilapidated		0·52
Percent of males in high status occupations	—·47	
Percent of separated males		0·46
Number of negroes		0·38
Percent of total labor force—female		0·33

SOURCE J. K. Hadden, The use of public transportation in Milwaukee, Wisconsin. The Eno Foundation for Highway Traffic Control, *Traffic Quarterly*, XVIII, No. 2, Table VI, 230 (1964).

Characteristics of the transportation system

The level of service offered by competing modes of transport is a critical factor in influencing modal split, whilst comparative journey times and out of pocket expenses for public and private transport facilities also influence the choice of travel mode. 1 *Relative travel time:* In the more recently developed modal split models relative travel time between competing modes has been found to influence modal choice. This travel-time ratio can be expressed as a time ratio of door-to-door travel time by public transport divided by the door-to-door travel time by private motor vehicle, e.g. the travel-time ratio developed by the National Capital Transportation Agency[8] is a typical travel-time ratio.

(Travel-time ratio) $\text{TTR} = \dfrac{X_1 + X_2 + X_3 + X_4 + X_5}{X_6 + X_7 + X_8}$

where $X_1 =$ Time spent in public transport vehicle.

$X_2 =$ Time spent changing from one public transport vehicle to another

$X_3 =$ Time spent waiting for public transport vehicle.

$X_4 =$ Time spent walking to public transport vehicle at origin.

X_5 Time spent walking from public transport vehicle at destination.

$X_6 =$ Time spent driving car.

$X_7 =$ Time spent parking vehicle at destination.

$X_8 =$ Time spent walking from parked vehicle to destination.

An alternative measure of relative travel time is the absolute difference between travel time by public transport and private motor vehicle and in Leeds this has been shown to be the more reliable measure.[9] However, a basic objection to the widespread use of the absolute difference in travel times is that it has a greater relative effect on the shorter trips. Figure 18 illustrates

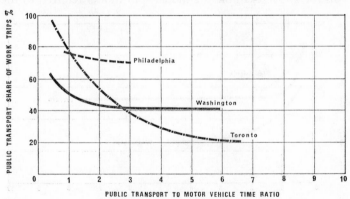

Fig. 18   Travel time ratio diversion curve for work trips in peak periods

SOURCE   Hill D. M., Von Cube H. G., Development of a model for forecasting travel mode choice in urban areas. *Highway Research Board, Record No. 38* (1963).

the effect of travel-time ratio on the public transport share of work trips in the peak hour.

2 *Relative travel cost:* The relative cost of travel between competing modes has been found to influence modal choice and this relative travel cost ratio can be expressed as the out-of-pocket travel cost by public transport, divided by the out-of-pocket cost by private motor vehicle. The relative travel-cost ratio developed by the National Capital Transportation Agency[10] is a typical example, where

$$(\text{Travel-cost ratio}) \ TCR = \frac{X_9}{(X_{10}+X_{11}+0\cdot5X_{12})/X_{13}}$$

where X_9 =Fare by public transport
X_{10}=Cost of petrol
X_{11}=Cost of oil
X_{12}=Cost of parking
X_{13}=Average car occupancy.

The other costs of running a motor vehicle, e.g. road tax, insurance are ignored as it has been found that drivers do not consider these costs when considering a particular journey.

In the above example the modal split model referred to the

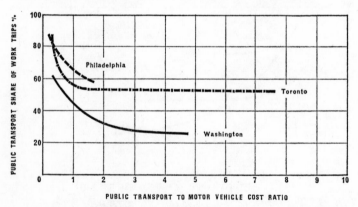

Fig. 19 Cost ratio diversion curve for work trips in peak periods

SOURCE   Hill D. M., Von Cube H. G., Development of a model for fore-casting travel mode choice in urban areas, *Highway Research Board, Record No. 38* (1963).

morning peak period only. To take account of the fact that it related to the one way cost of the journey only half of the parking costs have been included.

3 *Relative level of service:* The relative level of service offered by public and private transport is affected by a variety of factors— the majority of which are subjective and difficult to quantify, e.g. comfort, convenience, ease of changing from one mode to another. The measure of the relative level of service derived by the National Capital Transportation Agency is again fairly typical and is defined by a factor called excess travel time. That is time spent outside the vehicle (public or private) during a particular journey, e.g. walking, waiting, parking delay.

As a ratio it can be expressed

$$\text{(Travel-service ratio) TSR} = \frac{X_2 + X_3 + X_4 + X_5}{X_7 + X_8}$$

where X_2 = Time-spent changing between public transport vehicles

X_3 = Time spent waiting for a public transport vehicle

X_4 = Time spent walking to public transport vehicle at origin

X_5 = Time spent walking from public transport vehicle at destination

X_7 = Time spent parking car at destination

X_8 = Time spent walking from parking place to destination

4 *Accessibility indices:* In the more recently developed trip-end modal split models, such as the *Puget Sound* (1960) and the *Southeastern Wisconsin Regional Land Use Transportation Study* (1963) accessibility indices have been used as a measure of the quality of service provided by the alternate modes of transport. These indices measure the ease with which activity in one area can be reached from a particular zone on a specific transportation system, e.g. The accessibility from zone i to zone j is defined as the product of trip attractions in zone j multiplied by the friction factor for the zonal interchange. These products are then summed from zone i to all other zones in the area to obtain the accessibility index for zone i. The accessibility

index used by the *Southeastern Wisconsin Regional Land Use Transportation Study*[11] is typical and illustrates these points. Thus

$$Q_i = \sum_{j-1}^{n} A_j(F_{ij})$$

where Q_i =Accessibility index for zone i to all other zones (by public transport or motor vehicle)

A_j =Attractions in zone j (by public transport or private motor vehicle)

F_{ij} =Travel time friction factor for travel from zone i to zone j on the particular transportation system being considered

n =Total number of zones

The friction factor (F_{ij}) is equal to one divided by the door-to-door travel time, raised to some power b which varies with the travel time.

Thus

$$F_{ij} = \frac{1}{(\text{door-to-door travel time})^b}$$

Door-to-door travel time for motor vehicles includes walking at origin and destination, unparking and parking time, and driving time, whilst door-to-door travel time for public transport includes walking and waiting time at origin, time spent travelling on the vehicle, changing time between vehicles where applicable, walking time at destination. Relative travel service provided by two modes is measured by the ratio of the private motor vehicle accessibility index divided by the public transport accessibility index. This is referred to as the accessibility ratio.

Other transportation studies have used different indices of accessibility, e.g. *The London Traffic Survey*[12] accessibility index reflects the number of routes serving a zone, the frequency of service and the area of the zone. Thus the bus accessibility index was defined as

$$AI = \frac{\sum_i \sqrt{N_{ij}}}{\sqrt{A_j}}$$

where N_{ij} =Off-peak frequency of buses on route i and passing
through zone j

A_j =Area of the zone in square miles.

Similarly, the rail accessibility index was defined as

$$AI = \frac{\sum_i \sqrt{N_{ij}}}{A_j}$$

where N_{ij} =Number of trains during the off-peak period
stopping at station i in zone j.

The advantages claimed for these indices are that they are
simple, rational and easy to calculate. However, it can be
argued that they do not provide a completely satisfactory
measure of the relationship between one zone and another, e.g.
a zone of origin may have a very comprehensive and frequent
bus service within the zone, but may be linked only to the
central area, and, say, one other zone *en route*. Thus the accessibility of the origin zone to all other zones may be poor
despite a high level of service within the zone.

Choice and captive travellers

For each mode of travel there are two classes of traveller—
captive travellers and choice travellers. Captive travellers are
those with access to only one mode of travel for the bulk of
their trips. Thus non-car-owning households are generally
'captive' to public transport, whilst households in areas
removed from public transport routes are generally captive to
the motor vehicle. 'Choice' travellers are those with a choice of
different modes. Car ownership is perhaps the most significant
factor affecting whether a traveller is 'captive' or 'choice' and
logically enough the proportion of 'choice' travellers is greater
in large urban areas providing a range of public transport
facilities including, rail, underground and bus services.

Modal split in the transportation planning process

The procedure adopted for estimating modal split in the
transportation planning process varies with the type of model

used. A trip-end model allocates total person movements to alternate modes of travel before the trip distribution stage of the process, whilst trip interchange models allocate movements to the alternate modes after the total movements have been distributed between zones of origin and destination.

1 Trip-end modal split model: The general procedure adopted in trip-end modal split models is similar, although the journey purposes and variables used to determine the modal split often vary with the design and characteristics of different transportation studies. A typical trip-end modal split model might use four journey purposes, e.g. home-based work, shopping, social/recreational, and miscellaneous, and base its modal choice on a range of variables.

Using forecasted land-use and socio-economic data, total person trip productions and attractions are estimated for each zone for the base year, in the trip generation stage of the process.

The next stage in the process involves the allocation of total person trip productions to public transport for each journey purpose, by considering the attractiveness of the public transport system as measured by the variables considered to influence the modal split in the area under examination. This allocation is usually achieved through multiple linear regression techniques, and a typical equation might take the form

$$Y = a_0 + a_1 \log x_1 + a_2 \log x_2 + a_3 x_3 + a_4 x_4 + a_5 x_5 + a_6 x_6 + a_7 x_7$$

where Y = percentage of all journeys to work by public transport

x_1 = Travel-time ratio

x_2 = Travel-cost ratio

x_3 = Car ownership

x_4 = Family-size index

x_5 = Economic-class index

x_6 = Length of journey

x_7 = Percentage of females in employed population[13]

Journeys made by motor vehicle are derived by subtracting the estimated public transport trip productions from the total person trip production estimate.

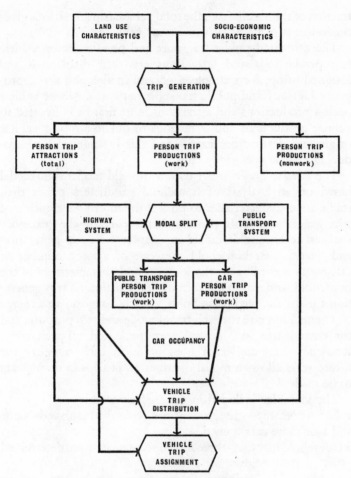

Fig. 20   Generalised trip-end modal split diagram

SOURCE   *Modal Split*, Bureau Public Roads, Washington (1966),

Future trip attractions by public transport are then estimated, usually by multiple linear regression techniques, using, for example, variables such as the location of the destination zone, the employment level in the zone, and the characteristics associated with the use of public transport in that zone. Subtraction of this figure from the total person trip attractions gives the journeys made by private motor vehicles.

The estimated public transport and private motor vehicle trip productions and attractions are then distributed and assigned using, for example, a gravity model, and the appropriate highway and public transport networks. Motor vehicle person productions and attractions must first be converted to vehicle productions and attractions to obtain a motor vehicle origin and destination matrix, and this is achieved by introducing vehicle occupancy rates.

The *London Traffic Survey* used a trip-end modal split model based on an analysis of household parameters rather than traffic zone characteristics to project the modal distribution of trip generation. This process forms part of the 'category analysis' technique described in Chapter 3 on trip generation and 'places each household into one of a large number of categories according to the location and characteristics of the household, and expresses from the information on trip generation for the sampled households in each category, an average trip generation rate for each travel mode and trip purpose, and for central area, non-central area, peak and off-peak trips. Knowing the number of households in each category for future years allows a modal distribution of trips in these years to be made.'[14]

The variables included in the analysis were:

1 Car ownership—three categories were distinguished—0, 1, and 2 or more cars owned

2 Household income—three income categories were determined

Low   £1,000

Medium   £1,000–£2,000 p.a.

High   £2,000

3 Employed Residents—three categories of household based on the number of employed residents—0, 1, and 2 or more employed residents

4 Rail Accessibility—three ranges of rail accessibility index were distinguished

Low   (0–10)

Medium   (10–25)

High   (25)

5 Bus accessibility—three ranges of bus accessibility index were distinguished

> Low   (0–8)
> Medium   (8–25)
> High   (25)

Future values of bus and rail accessibility were estimated by

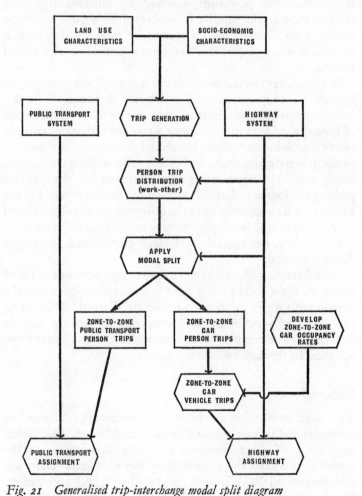

Fig. 21 Generalised trip-interchange modal split diagram

SOURCE   *Modal Split*, Bureau of Public Roads, Washington (1966).

examining past trends in the extension or retraction of bus routes, and in the case of rail by determining the amount of new rail construction likely under present transport policies.

2 *Trip-interchange modal split models:* Trip-interchange modal split models allocate journey movments to different modes after total person movements between pairs of zones have been distributed. The procedure adopted by different trip-interchange modal split models is similar, although they may be designed to operate with a particular type of distribution model, and use different variables to determine the modal choice.

A typical trip-interchange model designed, for example, to operate in conjunction with a gravity distribution model, would accept as input a zone to zone gravity model distribution of home-based person trips. From this input and using multiple linear regression techniques the model determines zone to zone public transport travellers, and motor vehicle trip interchanges, using variables representing characteristics of the persons making the journey, characteristics of the destination end of the journey, and characteristics of the transport system all measured on a zone to zone basis, e.g. relative travel time from door-to-door, income, net residential density, employment density at destination end.

By subtracting the public transport trips between pairs of zones from the total person trips between the same zones the person trips made by motor vehicle are derived. By dividing this total by appropriate car occupancy factors the vehicle interchanges between zones are determined, which can then be assigned to the highway network.

Conclusions

Two basic approaches can be used in estimating future public transport and private motor vehicle use, although the detailed application of either approach can vary significantly in the variables used and the journey purposes examined. There are advantages and disadvantages associated with both approaches. The trip-end approach to modal split, unlike trip-interchange, is capable of making separate public transport and private motor vehicle distributions between pairs of zones, and this is considered desirable because of the frequently differing lengths of journey by car and public transport. Thus the distribution of total person trips is often considered a basic weakness of trip-interchange models.

Another disadvantage associated with trip-interchange models is that with an increase in the number of zones used in the transportation study, the number of 'splits' required to determine modal choice for the area under study increases with the square of the number of zones used. There are disadvantages associated with the trip-end models, the most significant of which is that characteristics of the transportation system are fed into these models as average area-wide values. Thus the trip-end model is unable to reflect a particular zone to zone combination as precisely as trip-interchange models.

General criticisms of both types of models are based on the fact that present-day levels of service are used, which have a built-in bias in favour of the motorcar. Thus the situation could arise where future estimates of public transport usage could be on the low side if a substantially improved public transport system is developed by the base year, or if the road pricing and parking policies affect the use of the motor vehicle.

Despite the uncertainty associated with the determination of future modal choice, great advances have been made in the past ten years. However, little systematic knowledge exists on these matters, and considerable research, especially in the field of motivation studies, is required before it can be said that acceptable and reliable estimates of future modal split can be made.

References

1 *Chicago Area Transportation Study*, Final Report, Volumes 1 and 2 (1960).
2 Weiner E., A modal split model for Southeastern Wisconsin, Technical Records (Vol. II, No. 6) Southeastern Wisconsin Regional Planning Commission (1966).
3 National Capital Transportation Agency. A model for estimating travel mode usage. *Traffic Forecasting,* Vols. I, IV and V, Washington (1962).

4 See Wilson F. R., *The Journey to Work—Modal Split*, pages 119–170. Maclaren (1967).
5 National Capital Transportation Agency, *op. cit.*
6 Wilson F. R., *op. cit.*
7 Schwarz A., Forecasting transit use, *Highway Research Board*, Bulletin No. 297 (1961).
8 National Capital Transportation Agency, *op. cit.*
9 Quarmby D. A., Choice of travel mode for the journey to work, *Journal of Transport Economics and Policy* (1967).
10 National Capital Transportation Agency, *op. cit.*
11 Weiner E., *op. cit.*
12 Freeman, Fox, Wilbur Smith and Associates, *London Traffic Survey*, Vol. II (1966).
13 Wilson F. R., *op. cit.*
14 Freeman, Fox, Wilbur Smith and Associates, *op. cit.*

7 Computers in transportation planning

Introduction

Computers are an integral part of the transportation planning process, and over the past ten to twelve years advances in this field have invariably been paralleled with the evolution of digital computer technology. Without the aid of the computer, analysis of the large quantities of data collected would be so laborious and time-consuming, that it would not be attempted, whilst the solution of the different models and simulation processes can often only be satisfactorily completed by computer.

The first application of computers to the transportation planning process was concerned primarily with the tabulation of the extensive survey information collected, although as the size of core store increased, and the difficulties of programming were reduced the computer was used to solve the early trip distribution models such as the Fratar, and Detroit, growth factor models.

The most significant development in the field of traffic assignment by computer occurred in 1957 with the work of E. F. Moore[1] on the theory of switching. Further work by the Armour Research Foundation led to the development of a limited traffic assignment by computer, which was refined and ultimately applied by the staff of the Chicago Area Transportation Study to the entire Chicago metropolitan area. By 1962 the transportation planning process was served by a complete package of computer programmes covering distribution and assignment models, and complex data analysis. These programmes are well recorded and documented[2,3,4] and readily available to potential users. The development of larger computers, capable of carrying out calculations and data manipulation at very high speeds, has had a marked effect in the field of transportation planning. The development of simple programming languages such as Cobol and Fortran now allows the transportation planner to write his own programmes for specific jobs. Larger core storage facilities ensure that extensive and complex transportation networks can now be studied relatively easily. Faster and larger machines and easier programming have encouraged the development of different approaches to the same problems with the result that alternative models and procedures can be used for the different steps of the process.

Today the transportation planning process includes not only the analysis of survey data, and the estimation of future demand for trip making, but also the evaluation of alternative transport systems to derive priorities for construction and development. The mass of data, and the basic economic theory required to complete this evaluation, can only be handled satisfactorily by computer.

Computers

It is not the intention of this work to describe in detail computing techniques and languages. These are fully documented elsewhere.[5-7] However, to understand the relationship between computing technology and transportation planning it is necessary to outline the basic elements of a computer, and the method of giving instructions to the machine. There are two quite distinct families of computers—analogue computers and digital computers. In an analogue situation values are given some actual form as opposed to a numerical form, e.g. the speedometer of a motor car is analogue, the speeds are represented by the position of a pointer, and not by numerical digits. Similarly, the slide rule, the use of which involves the manipulation of lengths of wood, can be considered a simple form of analogue computer.

On the other hand digital processes work with numbers, alphabetical characters, and the usual arithmetical processes. Digital computers can store and manipulate numbers and alphabetical characters, and can be instructed to perform logical operations such as the solution of a mathematical problem.

Analogue computers have not as yet been applied to transportation planning, largely because of the complex nature of the models derived to predict trip generation, distribution, assignment and modal split, involving repetitious computation and data manipulation. For this reason, the application of only digital computers to transportation planning will be considered here.

The basic elements of the digital computer system are the central processing unit, which carries out the calculation required by a particular programme—and the peripherals—which are devices to put data into the computer and record the results. These peripheral devices are known as input and output devices. Because the central processing unit carries out the required calculations extremely rapidly—in millionths of a second—it is vital that both input and output devices should also operate as quickly as possible to achieve the fastest possible over-all rate of working.

Generally speaking, input and output media are divided into two categories, (1) slow-speed media which can be created and read manually, and (2) high-speed media which can only be created and read by the computer.

Input and output devices

Punched cards are perhaps the simplest form of computer record and because they are straightforward and long established are still very much in use. The standard card in use is the eighty-column card, which has twelve rows each with its numerical significance. Alphabetical characters are represented by a simple extension of the numeric code. They can be created and read manually.

Basic information is punched on to the cards in accordance with a predetermined coding system, and this information is transferred to and held by the central processor, by means of a card reader. A typical card reader can cope with 960 cards per minute, or approximately 1,000 characters per second, which, compared with other forms of input, is slow.

Punched cards can also be used to record output data, which is punched on a peripheral card punch unit at a rate of up to 450 characters per second.

A cheaper and more easily stored form of input record is punched paper tape, although it has the slight drawback of being more difficult to read manually. Data is punched on to 5, 6, 7, or 8 track paper tape and read into the computer by a paper tape reader at speeds of up to 1,000 characters per second. A character is represented by a pattern of holes marked off across the tape in a 'set' or 'frame'.

Paper tape can also be used to record output data in the same way as punched cards, although its speed of use in this connection is very slow—110 characters per second.

The magnetic tape reader is perhaps the principal high speed peripheral device. It can be used as a means of input and for recording output data. Data is recorded by magnetised spots in 'sets' or 'frames' across the magnetic tape, in much the same way as data is recorded on paper tape. A typical magnetic tape reader is capable of reading input data, or writing output data at a rate of 96,000 characters per second, which is considerably faster than using either cards or paper tape as direct input to the central processing unit. However, magnetic tape can only be created and read by the computer, and since the bulk of a computer's output must eventually take a form which can be read by man, the line printer, another 'peripheral', is an extremely important output device. This peripheral, in response to a programme instruction, normally prints a horizontal line of characters on stationery which is fed continuously through the machine. This stationery is 'spaced', i.e. the paper moves up one line before that line is printed. The number of printing positions in a line varies with the type of computing system and machine specification. Typical line printers have 96, 120 or 160 printing positions in one line, and on each of these printing positions any character from a range of numeric, alphabetic and special characters can be printed. A typical line printer will print out approximately 1,100 lines a minute if the full range of characters is required.

To avoid delaying the next calculation to be carried out by the central processing unit, the more recent line printers, rather than transferring the print line direct from the central processing unit to the print barrell, have an intermediate station incorporated. This stores the next line to be printed, whilst the line printer is printing the previous line, and the central processing unit continues with the assembly of the next line.

Magnetic discs are another means of supplying input data to and recording output data from the central processing unit. Each disc surface consists of a number of bands (typically, 200) and each band is capable of holding characters in a code of magnetised dots (typically, 1,680 characters). A number of discs are contained in a removable cartridge, and a computer installation may have any number of disc cartridges.

The reading of data from, or the recording of data to, such discs is as rapid as all but the fastest magnetic tape units (typically, 66,000 characters per second). They are convenient and simple to handle and store, and provide random access to any data stored, not just the next sequentially stored data. Magnetic discs are commonly used to hold data permanently on tap, and because of this are often called backing or second level storage.

Other forms of input and output device include the interrogating typewriter. This is a slow device which is used manually to enter messages with the central processor and which receives automatically typed replies.

The central processor

The central processing unit of any computing system comprises a storage medium in which data can be held and manipulated. It also holds the programme of instructions to be followed by the processing unit. A range of names has been used to describe the central processing unit's storage, but perhaps the most meaningful are core storage, magnetic core storage, and magnetic ferrite core storage. All three terms are based on the fact that the storage medium is composed of magnetic ferrite.

Purely numeric data can be held in the core storage by use of the binary number system, which takes the base 2. The numbers 1 or 0 are held in each position, and in excess of 1 a 'carry' forms to increase the next highest position. Thus instead of units, tens, hundreds, thousands, numbers are represented in the following way, for example:

32's	16's	8's	4's	2's	Units	
1	1	0	0	1	1	=51

Pure binary is simple and economical requiring that each unit of ferrite core store is in one of two positions 'on' or 'off'. Some digital computers are pure binary machines throughout, and such machines are designed for scientific work which requires only numeric answers. However, most problems requiring computer analysis also require alphabetic and decimal character data to pass through the computer unchanged. A simple method has been devised to allow this to take place by using a character code known as binary coded decimal. For each decimal digit four indicator positions are used, and each position may be either 'off' or 'on'. By utilising the different permutations of 'on' and 'off' it is possible to represent decimal characters. Thus

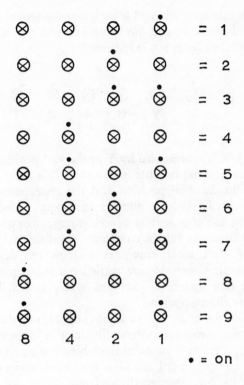

As with pure binary, the separate indicators in this computer code system are ferrite cores, and they are called bits. Each decimal character requires four bits, and in the above example the values 8421 have been given to the four bits.

As an alternative to a decimal character it is possible to hold an alphabetical character, but this involves the use of six bits per character instead of four. The two additional bits needed are given the 'value' X and Y.

Thus

The alphabetic code adopted is such that the letters A to I are represented by X in the 'on' position, and the appropriate decimal number from 1–9 is indicated, e.g.

$$B = \overset{\bullet}{\otimes} \quad \otimes \quad \otimes \quad \otimes \quad \overset{\bullet}{\otimes} \quad \otimes$$
$$ X \qquad Y \qquad 8 \qquad 4 \qquad 2 \qquad 1$$

Similarly J–R is represented by Y in the 'on' position and the appropriate decimal number 1–9, and S–Z is represented by X and Y in the 'on' position and the appropriate decimal number 1–9. To hold a number in binary coded decimal involves the use of more bits of core storage than pure binary. Thus to utilise to the full the core storage available in the Central Processing Unit most computer systems are designed so that arithmetic operations are carried out using pure binary, whilst for non-arithmetic purposes binary coded decimal is accepted by the computer.

To enable the computer to locate any item of data in core storage some computer systems divide it into compartments comprising a convenient number of binary bits, e.g. 8, 12 or 24. These compartments are known as *words*, and a computer which has its core storage divided into these distinct compartments is known as a fixed word length machine. Another method of locating data in core storage is to give an address to each character location or bit. Computers with this type of core storage are known as variable word length machines.

Programme instructions

As well as the data to be manipulated, core storage holds the programme of instructions to be followed by the processing units. These instructions are made up of characters or binary numbers just like the data to be manipulated and each instruction has a pattern known as the *instruction format*. A typical instruction format could consist of an operation code (e.g. add, subtract) and give the address of both items of data to be

176

operated on. The computer operates by continuously alternating between analysing the next instruction and obeying that instruction. The more advanced computers hold a specially prepared 'master' programme in core storage, to carry out many functions which would otherwise require detailed programming. This master programme, which is known as the *Executive*, is a series of sub-routines (or elements of a programme) using the instructions to which the computer is designed to respond, and amongst other functions it is responsible for the allocation of core storage. Before programme instructions can be understood by the central processing unit, they must be in the form of pure binary or binary coded decimal. Programmes written in this way are said to be in machine language. This type of programming language is clumsy and difficult for the average person to use. To overcome this programming languages which are more compatible with verbal and mathematical statements have been developed, e.g. Fortran, Cobol, and the central processing unit is supplied with a special programme called an assembler which can translate these high-level languages into machine language. Thus to write a computer programme, a knowledge of a high-level language such as Fortran, is all that is required. Once written it is fed into the processing unit, compiled, and checked for errors by the assembler. When all programme errors have been eliminated the programme is run using test data to check the logic of the programme of instructions.

Before preparing programme instructions for the computer analysis of a particular problem it is usual to set out the problem and its solution in the form of a flow chart, which follows certain diagramming conventions. The object is to define and represent the problem as a series of logical steps capable of solution. Once this is completed it is a comparatively simple matter to convert the flow chart into a language which the computer can understand.

Standard Programmes

Numerous standard programmes exist to produce a solution to a given problem in a quick and efficient way, and to save the non-expert programmer from struggling to write an inefficient programme to solve the same problem. These programmes are written by experts, for a particular computer system, and they are restricted to common problems which are widely encountered in the particular field of study, e.g. in transportation planning standard programmes exist for trip generation, trip distribution, traffic assignment, modal split and the economic evaluation of alternative networks. These programmes are made available by the various computer manufacturers in the form of library or monitor tapes.

To run a standard programme it is necessary to input data to the central processor through an input peripheral. The detail and format of the input will vary with the type of computer system used. However, the basic elements of the input are similar and in general terms consist of details of the problem being processed, programme instructions and the data to be processed. The details of the job involved include the identification of the user and the job; the calling into storage of any routines or sub-routines required, and the setting up of any peripheral devices to be used by the programme, e.g. line printer, paper tape reader. These details are generally input from punched cards or paper tape.

The programme instructions, setting out the process to be undertaken by the central processor, are then input from punched cards, paper tape or magnetic tape. If the programme already exists on magnetic tape, it is simply called into storage by the job control data. The end of the programme instructions is indicated by an identifying card (if the input is from punched cards) or data block, and this is followed by the data to be manipulated. The end of the data, and the end of the job is identified by an END card or data block.

Survey analysis

This type of standard programme has been developed to analyse the extensive and complex data collected in the survey stage of the process and to present it in a form that enables intelligible patterns to be discerned. Prior to the development of the computer, this data had to be processed manually, or by using simple punched card tabulators. Consequently severe limitations were imposed on the type of study which could be undertaken. Now, using a computer and a general survey analysis programme, the transportation planner needs only to specify the type of analysis required in a stylised form of English. The assembler then converts these instructions into a form which can be understood by the computer.

The basic data collected during the survey is punched on to cards or paper tape, depending on the type of input used in the computer system and in accordance with a predetermined coding system. It is essential that this coding be kept as straightforward as possible, to keep the cost of checking punching and coding errors to a minimum. Wherever possible three simple rules should be followed: (1) use numeric decimal coding, (2) use continuous code ranges, e.g. if the design of the study involves the use of eight journey purposes then these should be coded 0–7 and (3) use a most significant digit to indicate breaks in sequence, e.g. external traffic zones are characteristically prefixed by the digit 9..., internal zones by 1... and central area zones by 0.

Different computer systems have developed their own standard programmes, which vary in detail. In general terms, however, the procedures followed are similar.

The analysis of the basic data can most conveniently be considered in three stages. In the first stage it may be edited or added to in various ways, e.g. arithmetic operations can be performed on the data, whilst alterations can be made to the notations used. The basic records may also be subjected to checks to establish the relevance and validity of the variables used against a range of values for the same variables, which are specified by the user.

In the second stage, basic tables are formed from selected information in the basic data. These tables can take the form of general exploratory tables, or more detailed analysis of specific problems. Exploratory tables could, for example, analyse trip purpose only, irrespective of interzonal movements, to determine which trip purposes warrant further, more detailed analysis. At this stage the data can be manipulated and operated on, e.g. the rows and columns of separate tables can be joined

179

or merged, or arithmetic operations may be performed on individual rows and/or columns.

The third stage involves the output of the tables produced in stage two. Appropriate headings, text, row and column labels and other annotations are added. The analysed data can be output as 'printout', punched cards or paper tape, or magnetic tape, according to the requirements of the total transportation model. Throughout the analysis reports and error messages are provided on the interrogating typewriter.

Trip generation

Two basic methods are now in use to forecast trip generation—multiple linear regression and category analysis. Multiple linear regression standard programmes are generally available for most computer systems, but to date the only standard programme available for category analysis has been written for the Control Data 3300 computer.[8]

The details of regression standard programmes vary with the computer system used but in outline the procedure used is similar, and can be broken down into three stages:

1 The first step is the reading in of the basic data on which subsequent analyses are to be performed. This data must be stored in a manner which allows the subsequent analyses to take place. Consequently this stage of the programme provides for the transformation of this data into, for example, cross-product or correlation matrices from which regression analysis can proceed. Progress reports and error messages can usually be printed out at this stage.

2 The regression analysis is then performed on the transformed data derived in stage (1). Usually this standard programme is extremely flexible in application, and allows the user to carry out analysis with a dependent variable (Y) and a complete set or sub-set of independent variables (X_n). Appropriate confidence limits can be specified for the independent variables and if these are not met, then the 'offending' variables are eliminated from the set or sub-set.

3 The final stage of the programme involves the print out of the results of the transformations carried out in stage (1) and

the analysis performed in stage (2) with appropriate statistical measures of the quality of fit of the regression plane, e.g. standard error of estimate; multiple correlation co-efficient. Appropriate headings, text, and annotations are also added.

Category analysis is a new technique of estimating trip generation rates by mode of travel and journey purpose, using measured trip rates current today and a minimum of land-use and planning data. Indeed the information required about socio-economic characteristics is compatible with that available from the 1966 10% Sample Census.

The standard programme written for the CDC 3300 computer calculates person trip productions and attractions in each traffic zone, or group of zones, for three modes of travel and six journey purposes. The programme can be used to make predictions for any future year and for any land-use plan for which the appropriate data is available.

Trip distribution

The problem of estimating future inter-zonal traffic flows is of great importance in the transportation planning process, and numerous models have been developed to distribute these inter-zonal movements. However, two basic distribution models tend to be widely used and standard programmes are generally available for them. They are the gravity model and a growth factor model known as the Furness forecasting method.

The standard programmes for the Furness method can be basically subdivided into three stages:

1 *Input Stage*—which reads in and stores the data necessary for the subsequent computational procedures. The input data required consists of an origin and destination matrix of the existing traffic flows from one zone to all other zones. Normally, origin and destination data output on magnetic tape by the survey analysis standard programmes for a particular computer system will be accepted as input for the Furness distribution model standard programmes, written for the same computer system.

In addition to the origin and destination matrix, estimates of the future growth of traffic productions and attractions must also be supplied.

2 *Computation stage*—which calculates future flows between zones by an iterative process in which the sum of all traffic movements is made to agree alternatively with estimates of future traffic originating and terminating in each zone, until both estimates are satisfied or 'in balance'. Using this method the predicted trip interchanges retain approximately the same proportion of trips produced by the originating zone and attracted by the terminating zone.

It is normal to specify at the Input Stage the number of iterations or percentage accuracy required from the computational stage of the programme.

3 *Output stage*—which prints out, or records, the output from the Furness distribution model standard programme and takes the form of an origin and destination matrix of future interzonal movements, with the required headings and annotations.

The gravity model is possibly the most widely used and best documented trip distribution model and has a whole range of standard computer programmes available. The input required for the basic gravity model recommended by the Bureau of Public Roads, U.S.A.[9] consists of

1 trip productions and attractions for each zone, usually by journey purpose. At the calibration stage this data is derived from the observed origin and destination matrix. When future zonal trip interchanges are forecast, however, this information is derived from the trip generation stage of the process

2 minimum path travel times between zones, including time spent travelling within the zone of origin and destination. (Minimum time path routes from one zone centroid to all others are referred to as a 'tree'.) This information is normally derived from the 'tree-building' programme associated with the traffic assignment stage of the process

3 initial or assumed travel-time factors for each one minute increment of travel time

Before the gravity model can be used to forecast future trip interchanges it has to be made to fit the present-day situation.

This fitting procedure is known as calibration, and in outline involves the

1 calculation of present-day trip interchanges using the gravity model formula, data concerning zonal trip productions and attractions derived from the observed O and D matrix, and the initial, assumed, travel times

2 comparison between the number of trips attracted to each zone as derived from the gravity model, and the observed number of attractions extracted from the original origin – destination data. If there is any discrepancy between the two sets of figures then the programme adjusts the zonal trip attractions by a process of iteration, using the ratio of observed trips to calculated trips

3 calculation of a new set of trip interchanges using the adjusted zonal trip attractions

When the trip length frequency curves* derived from observed and estimated zonal interchanges are in close agreement the gravity model is said to be calibrated, and ready for use to predict future zonal trip interchanges using future estimates of zonal trip productions and attractions derived from the trip generation stage of the process.

If the comparisons are not in close agreement then adjustments are made to the initial travel-time factors by multiplying the travel-time factor used by the ratio of the percentage of survey trips to the percentage of estimated trips derived from the gravity model. This calculation results in a new set of travel-time factors, which are then used in place of the initial set of travel-time factors. The process of calibration is repeated until a satisfactory comparison of trip length distribution curves is achieved, and the model can then be used to predict future zonal trip interchanges.

Other types of gravity model use different measures of travel resistance in their basic structure, e.g. straight line or road distance between zone centroids is often used instead of travel-

* Trip length frequency curves take the form of a graph, with the percentage of total trips plotted against travel time, or distance. In the calibration stage of a gravity model programme they can be considered to be in close agreement when (i) visual inspection reveals a close relationship, and (ii) when the difference between average trip lengths is ± 3%.

time factors. However, the basic standard computer programme procedure involved with the Bureau of Public Roads gravity model can be considered typical.

Traffic assignment

Traffic assignment attempts to predict how a given volume of traffic is or will be distributed over the road system of a town or urban area. To date, two methods of assignment have standard computer programmes available for use with a range of computer systems. These are 'capacity restraint' and 'all or nothing'.

1 Capacity restraint

In general terms the capacity restraint programme requires as input (1) a description of the road network in terms of zone centroids, links and nodes (this description should include link speeds and capacity and traffic volumes), (2) future estimates of zonal trip interchanges in the form of an origin and destination matrix.

The operations then carried out by the programme are (1) the calculation of minimum paths between zone centroids, a procedure referred to as 'build trees', (2) the loading of inter-zonal trips to the minimum path 'trees' in specified percentage increments, and for a specified number of iterations.

Following the specified number of iterations the programme then takes account of vehicle interaction on the network, and calculates new travel speeds for all roads, according to the assigned traffic volume, link speeds and capacities. Using the new link travel speeds the minimum path trees are calculated. These are not necessarily the same as the previously used trees because of the introduction of new travel speeds on the links of the network, (3) the loading of the remaining inter-zonal movements to the network using the new 'trees', in specified percentage increments, and for a specified number of iterations. This procedure is followed until all the inter-zonal trip interchanges have been assigned to the network.

The output available from such a standard programme is

comprehensive, but is rarely asked for in its entirety because certain of its aspects are expensive of computer time. For each assignment directional traffic volumes, overloading and turning traffic on each link can normally be requested. Traffic routes from each zone can change with each iteration, and these changes can be printed out if required. However, the number of routes tends to be large, with the result that only certain routes are selected for printing out in this manner.

In addition to printing the route, standard programmes generally print the increment in traffic using the route, and the total time. However, route printing is expensive of computer time and its use is mainly confined to selected link assignments.

Other information such as total vehicle miles, total vehicle hours, average vehicle speed, is also normally included in the print out.

2 *All or nothing assignment*

The input required for a standard programme for all or nothing assignments is similar to that required for capacity restraint; (1) a description of the network in terms of zone centroids, links and nodes, including link travel speeds; (2) an origin and destination matrix derived from the survey analysis stage if existing flows are to be assigned, or from the trip distribution stage if estimated future zonal interchanges are to be assigned.

The programme operates by calculating minimum path trees between zones, then loading interzonal movements to these paths.

The output produced can include journey times between zones, minimum path trees, total turning movements, and the loadings on individual links. It is only on inspection of individual link loadings that 'overloads' are revealed, and this problem is overcome by revising the link travel speeds on the appropriate links, and re-running the programme until an acceptable assignment is produced.

Existing procedures for estimating choice of travel mode are fairly simple in concept, mainly because of a fundamental lack of understanding of behavioural characteristics. A range of modal split models are in use,[10] but the standard programmes available are restricted to the multiple linear regression and category analysis programmes already described.

Future developments

The field of computer technology is changing and advancing rapidly. Faster and larger machines are being developed, and in transportation planning this development is likely to be utilised in two ways—by testing more alternative transport network proposals or by developing more complex models to explain and predict future travel demands. It seems desirable that as many alternative networks as possible should be tested, but at the same time there is a case for developing more complex models, on the grounds that it is difficult, if not impossible, to explain a complex situation in terms of a simple model. However, 'it is important to ensure that the temptations offered by faster and bigger computers do not lead to overcomplicated procedures which add little to the quality or significance of the end products'.[11]

Larger core storage facilities, or the development of bulk storage, should allow a more detailed network coding of public transport systems. Indeed, it should be possible eventually to code highway, bus and rail systems in one network, which in turn should allow a more complex modal split procedure to be developed.

In the short term the development of computer time sharing will allow small concerns access to large computers, which they otherwise might not have had, whilst the experience gained by the various transportation planning consultants in recent years is likely to give rise to the development of standard packages for synthesising future travel patterns. A typical example of such a package is Synth developed by Scott, Wilson, Kirkpatrick and Partners.[12]

References

1 Moore E. F., The shortest path through a maze, International Symposium on the Theory of Switching, *Proceedings of the Harvard Society* (1957).
2 Manual of Procedures for a Home-Interview Traffic Study, *U.S. Department of Commerce, Bureau of Public Roads*, Washington (1954).
3 Traffic Assignment Manual, *U.S. Department of Commerce, Bureau of Public Roads*, Washington (1964).
4 Calibrating and testing a gravity model for any size urban area, *U.S. Department of Commerce, Bureau of Public Roads*, Washington (1965).
5 Whitworth D., *Basic Digital Computer Concepts*, Heinemann, London (1965).
6 Clay-Sprowls R., *Computers—A Programme Problem Approach*, Harper International Edition, Harper and Row, New York (1966).
7 Ledley R. S., *Fortran IV Programming*, McGraw-Hill (1966).
8 Freeman, Fox, Wilbur Smith and Associates, *Transport Analysis Programs*—System Guide 3 Category Analysis.
9 Calibrating and testing a gravity model for any size urban area, *op. cit.*
10 Modal split, *U.S Department of Commerce, Bureau of Public Roads*, Washington (1966).
11 Martin B. V., Use of the computer in transportation planning, *Journal of the Institution of Highway Engineers*, Vol. XV, 8 (1968).
12 Hodgen R. and Watson M., A rapid method for the synthesis of urban traffic, *Traffic Engineering and Control* (1968).

8 Economic evaluation of transportation proposals

Proposals to improve or extend existing transportation systems can range from limited improvements, such as the widening of a section of road, or the improvement of a junction, to comprehensive proposals which involve the construction of significant sections of urban motorway, the development of new forms of public transport, and the close integration of different transport systems. Before decisions are taken to proceed with any proposals, either small or large, an attempt is normally made to evaluate the efficiency of the proposed improvements. The large-scale transportation proposals are invariably assessed by means of a cost-benefit analysis, which aims to compare the costs and benefits associated with alternative schemes. This usually takes the form of an indication of the annual rate of return on the investment proposed, which is derived from a discounted benefit-cost calculation. The smaller scale proposals are generally assessed by less sophisticated methods, and in accordance with Ministry recommended procedures. Again the comparison of costs and benefits is indicated by a rate of return on the investment proposed, based on a simple annual rate of return.

Cost-benefit analysis

'Cost-benefit analysis is a practical way of assessing the desirability of projects, where it is important to take the long view (in the sense of looking at repercussions in the further, as well as the nearer, future) and a wide view (in the sense of allowing for side effects of many kinds on many persons, industries, regions), i.e. it implies the enumeration and evaluation of all the relevant costs and benefits.'[1]

Cost-benefit analysis is a technique which has been developed predominantly in this century, as an aid to decision making. It is basically a procedure to test the soundness of proposed developments by estimating the cost of a particular proposal, in terms of the value of the resources to be employed in the venture, and comparing these costs with the value of the goods or services produced by the development—the benefits.

In a market economy, where the value of any benefits associated with a particular venture are reflected in the price the consumer is prepared to pay, there is no need to carry out a cost-benefit analysis to decide the most appropriate course of action. However, there is a whole range of developments in our present society for which no direct charge is made, but which are essential to the economic and social well-being of the nation, e.g. schools, hospitals, transportation systems. Such developments or services are group or collective wants, which cannot be easily marketed, with the result that they are invariably paid for indirectly through taxation, and decisions to proceed with a particular venture at the expense of an alternative are often politically motivated. In general terms, guidance as to the policies to be adopted in connection with the provision of these services is obtained at the ballot box in Central and Local Government elections. However, this has resulted in many public expenditure decisions being taken by rule of thumb methods, which have led to the neglect of certain types of proposal such as road improvements, whilst in other spheres public money has been lavished with only the vaguest idea of the returns to be expected.

An increasing awareness of this problem on the part of

politicians and economists has resulted in a search for 'tools of economic appraisal to assess the wisdom of alternative courses of action that will be better than political decisions where a market is not, or can not, be used'.[2]

Pioneering work on cost-benefit analysis was carried out in the United States of America in connection with navigational improvement schemes following the River and Harbour Act 1902. At this stage the benefits were considered to be the value of additional commerce resulting from the improvement, whilst the costs were the actual capital costs of the improvement.

In the thirties, with the 'New Deal' philosophy and the idea of a broader social justification for proposed developments, the cost-benefit analysis technique was further advanced in the field of flood control schemes carried out under the Flood Control Act of 1936. Under this Act Federal aid was granted to such schemes 'if the benefits, to whom-so-ever they may accrue, are in excess of the estimated costs'. By 1945 the approach to cost-benefit analysis had been further broadened to include both indirect costs and benefits, and an assessment of intangible factors associated with development projects. This process of refining the basic techniques associated with cost-benefit analysis has continued to the present day.

In the field of transport, cost-benefit analysis was first used in the State of Oregon in 1938, in connection with road improvements and a great deal of work has now accumulated on the subject. In this country it has culminated in the thorough but traditional M1 and Victoria Line analyses. A more controversial approach to cost-benefit analysis, which attempts to take into account the many intangible social factors associated with transport and traffic schemes appeared in Appendix 2 of the Buchanan Report *Traffic in Towns*.

General principles of cost-benefit analysis

Cost-benefit analysis attempts to list the costs and benefits associated with the factors which need to be taken into account in making decisions about projects, whose value cannot be assessed in the open market. However, this simple aim poses

three main questions which are extremely difficult to answer:
1 Which costs and benefits are to be included in the analysis?
2 What value is to be placed on these costs and benefits?
3 At what rate of interest are these costs and benefits to be discounted?

In addition these questions must be answered within the physical, political, administrative and financial context of the time, with the result that a whole series of constraints must be considered to be operating on the process.

In general terms the procedure to be followed involves:
1 the definition of the project and the listing of the current costs and benefits to be included. The direct costs and benefits to the sponsor of the project are usually defined quite simply, e.g. the costs could involve the amount of capital tied up in the project, the labour force required to implement the proposals, whilst the benefits could take the form of increased productivity and profits. However, there is another group of costs and benefits which accrue to persons or bodies other than the one sponsoring the project. These external effects are often difficult to identify and manifest themselves in many different ways, e.g. a typical external benefit could result from the construction of a dam to generate electricity which also gives flood protection which is not paid for by those receiving it. A typical external cost could result from atmospheric and water pollution associated with an industrial process.
2 the placing of a monetary value on the costs and benefits associated with the project, in order to arrive at an estimate of the current net benefit. Where the costs and benefits involved can be expressed in monetary terms, all the values used must be reckoned on the same basis, which is usually the level of the market prices prevailing in the initial year. Problems arise, however,

    a when the scale of the project is large enough to affect these prices. In such instances it is normal practice to assume a linear relationship between the original and ultimate levels, and adopt a value halfway between the two
    b when monopoly conditions exist, and distort relative outputs away from those which would prevail under conditions of perfect competition. Accounting adjustments can be

made by applying a correction to the actual level of costs *c* when intangible costs and benefits, which cannot be quantified, are involved in the analysis, e.g. the scenic effect of building electricity transmission lines.

3 The choice of an appropriate rate of interest to compare the stream of annual net benefits with the capital cost of the project. Bearing in mind that the function of a rate of interest is to allocate capital funds between the varying uses to which they might be put, and to reflect society's preferences between present and future consumption, the choice of an appropriate rate of interest is purely value judgement.

In short the 'most that can be said for the doctrine (of cost–benefit analysis) is that by listing the supposed indirect benefits or detriments, it indicates a desire to introduce a semblance of rationality into the spending of large sums of money by public authority'.[3]

Examples of cost-benefit analysis in transportation planning

The M1 motorway study[4]

The M1 study, which was published in 1960, was the first major cost-benefit analysis undertaken in the transportation planning field in the United Kingdom. The study was carried out in two main parts (*a*) an investigation of the traffic implications of the motorway, and (*b*) an economic assessment of the traffic implications.

The traffic investigation included an estimate of the number of vehicles of different types which could be expected to divert to the motorway; the journey time and mileage savings involved for this diverted traffic; and the likely changes in the number and type of accidents as a result of the new motorway facility.

The implications of these predicted changes in the traffic characteristics were then examined by economists, who defined their task as the measurement of 'the hypothetical sum that the community would be prepared to pay for the motorway rather than not have it'.[5] In deriving this hypothetical sum, Beesley and Reynolds, the economists involved, examined

1 the benefits to traffic diverted to the motorway
2 the benefits resulting from reduced congestion on the existing road network
3 the benefits derived from the change in accident characteristics
4 the benefits to traffic which was estimated would be induced to travel because of the lower cost of travel after the motorway was constructed. This type of traffic is referred to as generated traffic.

The study found that the major benefit likely to be derived from the construction of the M1 was a reduction in journey time, and it was assumed that changes in the amount of time spent by vehicle occupants travelling as part of their work could be valued at the average hourly earnings of the persons involved. Journeys other than those carried out in connection with employment were more difficult to value. To overcome this problem a range of assumed values was adopted for leisure time savings.

Another benefit assumed to derive from a reduction in the time taken to complete a journey was the reduction in the size of vehicle fleets necessary to carry the same ton mileage. This assumption is open to criticism on the grounds that given fixed working hours, and vehicle operating regulations, small changes in journey time would not be sufficient to allow the same vehicle to make additional journeys.

Further benefits were assumed, resulting from changes in fuel consumption, and vehicle operating costs, and an estimate of the annual value of the reduction in accidents resulting from the construction and use of the motorway. Changes in fuel consumption were calculated net of tax on the grounds that indirect taxation merely represents a transfer from one sector of the community to another, whilst the valuation of accidents was based on a consideration of loss of output, medical expenses, damage to property and administrative expenses.[6]

Benefits received by generated traffic, which came into existence only because of the reduced costs of road transport, were considered to be of less importance than existing journeys which were being made at the original higher level of transport costs. Consequently they were valued at half the average benefits per vehicle mile experienced by the existing traffic.

This type of analysis of the benefits associated with the construction of the M1 did not take into account external effects such as changes in the environmental standards, which cannot readily be quantified or valued.

The financial cost of the construction of the M1, estimated at £23·3m, was considered to be a reasonable measure of cost, which included the opportunity cost (or alternative benefits rejected). The annual rate of return on the capital invested was used as the simplest method of comparing costs and benefits. Table 3 illustrates the estimated net annual savings to be derived from the construction of the M1.

Table 3. *Estimated savings and increases in annual costs resulting from construction of the M1 motorway.*

	Changes in £000's per annum	
	Benefit	Cost
Savings in working time by traffic transferring to motorway	453	
Reduction in vehicle fleets	80	
Change in fuel consumption for vehicle mileage transferred to motorway	117	
Change in other operating costs of vehicle mileage transferred	200	
Cost of additional vehicle mileage incurred in transferring to motorway		229
Reductions in cost to vehicles remaining on old roads	128	
Benefits for generated traffic	113	
Savings in non-work hours (dependent on hourly rate chosen)	0–938	
Reduction in accidents	215	
Maintenance costs of motorway		200
Totals	1306–2244	429
Net Annual Savings per annum	877–1815	

SOURCE *The London–Birmingham Motorway—Traffic and Economics.* Road Research Technical Paper No. 46., H.M.S.O.

The annual rate of return derived from this analysis varied with the hourly rate assumed for non-working time (which ranged from zero to 10s. per hour). If non-working time was valued at zero the annual rate of return was found to be 3·8% at 6s. per hour it was 6·2%, and at 10s. per hour it was 7·8%.

The Victoria Line cost-benefit analysis[7,8]

The Victoria Line analysis undertaken by the Road Research Laboratory and the London Transport Board marked an important advance in the development of cost-benefit techniques by attempting to take into account the value of social benefits derived from the construction of the Victoria Line underground railway. On a purely commercial basis the Victoria Line was an extremely unattractive proposition, which at the then current fare levels was estimated by Foster and Beesley to be likely to run at a loss of £2·14m per annum. However, they went on to argue that the benefits likely to be derived from (1) the reduction in journey time and costs, and the improved comfort and convenience experienced by those persons diverted to the Victoria Line, (2) the reduction in journey time and vehicle operating costs experienced by those not diverting to the Victoria Line, (3) the generated traffic attracted to the Victoria Line which would not otherwise have travelled—must all be considered in an attempt to assess whether the benefits associated with the project were in excess of the costs likely to be incurred.

Two values for time were used in assessing the benefits likely to be derived from reduced journey times—a value for work time and a value for non-work time. The work time value was based on a sample of the hourly wage rate of those likely to be affected by the Victoria Line (7s. 3d. per hour) whilst the non-work time value was taken somewhat arbitrarily at 5s. per hour. It was estimated that 95% of the journey time savings would be derived in non-work time.

The improved comfort and convenience likely to be associated with the Victoria Line were imputed indirectly, by estimating and giving a value to the increased probability of getting a seat on the Victoria Line. Foster and Beesley argue that given a valuation of time, and observing how many people chose to transfer from a fast service with low seating probability to a slower service with a better seating probability a value can be set on the rate of substitution of comfort for time. Rather than use the yearly return on outlayed capital as a crude measure of costs and benefits the present discounted net value was used to express the comparison of costs and benefits. The reasoning behind the choice of this method was that it takes several years to construct an underground railway over which time the capital cost of construction is spent. But for this same period of time no benefits will result until the line (or sections of it) are completed. Thus a method of evaluation is required which takes account of the time at which the costs and benefits accrue, and the most appropriate was considered to be the present discounted net value.

Table 4. *Victoria Line—Social Benefit and Loss (Five and a half years' construction, and fifty years' life assumed.)*

	Present discounted value at 6% £m
(A) Costs—Annual working expenses	16·16
(B) Benefits—Traffic diverted to Victoria Line from private motor vehicle, buses, and underground, including time and comfort savings.	29·34
(C) Traffic not diverted to Victoria Line (includes comfort and time savings for bus, rail, motor vehicle and underground).	44·79
(D) Generated traffic, includes time, fare and other savings	11·74
(E) Terminal scrap value	0·29
(F) Total Benefits (B+C+D+E)	86·16
(G) Net current benefit (F−A)	70·00
(H) Value of Capital expenditure	38·81
(I) Net Benefit (G−H)	31·19
(J) Social surplus rate of return	11.3%

source Foster C. D., and Beesley M. E., Estimating the social benefit of constructing an underground railway in London, *Journal of the Royal Statistical Society* (Series A 1963).

For the purposes of the study a range of discount factors was taken, i.e. 8%, 6% and 4%. Using the 6% factor as an example it simply means that £1 benefit realised today is equivalent to £1·06 of benefit in one year's time. Assuming a fifty-year operating period for the line and using this discount factor, both benefits and costs in the future were discounted back to the time of the study.

Table 4 sets out the costs and benefits measured by Foster and Beesley using the 6% discount factor, and expresses the total as an annual rate of return of 11·3% over the period of construction and operation on the present value of the capital invested.

General criticisms of the method adopted are (1) it does not take into account all the social consequences, (2) the valuations were undertaken in the context of current vehicle taxes and fare levels.

Cost-benefit analysis, and accessibility and environment

The Buchanan Report expressed the relationship between accessibility, environment and cost in the form of a rough and ready law: 'In any environmental area, if a certain standard of environment is adhered to, the level of accessibility that can be obtained depends on the amount of money that can be spent on physical alterations.'[9]

Having stated this 'law' the report outlines a technique which allows the three variables—environment, accessibility and cost —to be measured so that qualities of different highway networks can be compared, and the most efficient arrangement identified. However, environment and accessibility as defined in the report are comprised largely of intangible and unquantifiable elements, such as comfort, convenience, appearance, which are difficult if not impossible to value.

In an attempt to illustrate how this problem could be overcome the report took Newbury as a case study, listed all the important identifiable benefits associated with the three alternative town centre schemes put forward, and attempted to give them a numeric value to represent their various qualities. The costs of the three different proposals were measured in

197

terms of the net capital cost of preparing land for building, i.e. cost of acquisition, clearing and servicing minus the value of the land for building purposes. The cost of building was excluded on the assumption that at the time of development the cost of the buildings is equal to their value if cost is taken to include the developers' profit, so that their net cost is nil.

The benefits associated with the accessibility were considered under

1 the safety of the layout for vehicle operation (40)
2 the distribution of parking and loading facilities (25)
3 the suitability of internal routes to allow direct access from one area to another (20)
4 the convenience of the layout for vehicle users (15).

The maximum numeric values given to each of these aspects were 40, 25, 20 and 15 respectively, and a subjective assessment made of the weighting warranted by each town centre scheme. From this an Index of Accessibility was derived. The benefits associated with environment were considered under the safety, comfort, convenience and appearance of the particular area for the people living and working there. Again the respective maximum numeric values were 60, 15, 15 and 10, and subjective assessments were made of the appropriate weighting to be given to each alternative town centre scheme. Using these weightings an Index of Environment was derived.

The next stage of the process involved the calculation of one index to reflect both the level of environment and accessibility for each scheme (the Index of Environment and Accessibility). These indices were then compared with the Index of Environment and Accessibility derived for the present-day situation to obtain a measure of the benefits associated with the alternative schemes. The measure of each benefit was then related to the cost of implementing the scheme (i.e. benefit divided by cost) to represent a rate of return on the investment.

Table 5 illustrates the relative costs and benefits associated with the three alternative proposals for Newbury. On cost grounds alone scheme B has the highest rate of return, and should be implemented. However, there is a need to decide whether the extra benefits derived from scheme B warrant the additional expenditure over scheme A.

Table 5. *Benefits and Costs—Newbury*

Scheme	Index of environment and accessibility	Benefit	Cost	Benefit/Cost
No change	11	nil	nil	0
(A) Limited improvements	22	11	2·7	4·1
(B) Improved primary network	57	46	3·4	13·5
(C) Improved primary network and internal circulation	72	61	5·6	10·9

SOURCE   Appendix 2, *Traffic in Towns*, H.M.S.O. (1963)

This is achieved by relating the incremental costs to the additional benefits derived to obtain a measure of the rate of return on the extra cost involved.

Table 6. *Incremental costs and benefits—Newbury.*

Scheme	Additional benefit	Incremental cost	Benefit/cost
		(£m)	
No change	—	—	—
(A)	11	2·7	4
(B)	35	0·7	50
(C)	15	2·2	7

SOURCE   Appendix 2, *Traffic in Towns*, H.M.S.O. (1963)

Table 6 shows that in the Newbury case study scheme B, which costs £0·7m more than scheme A, has an increased Index of Environmental Accessibility of 35, and the rate of return on the additional investment is 50. Thus scheme B on both its benefit/cost ratio, and incremental benefit/cost ratio has the highest rate of return.

This technique can be criticised on the gounds that it is subjective, and the allocation of numeric values arbitrary. However, in its favour it does attempt to take account of the many external factors which are difficult to quantify, whilst with time and when sufficient schemes have been examined in this way a consensus of opinion could well develop about the weighting system to be adopted. In the words of the Report 'however immature the analysis technique may be at this stage, its use will lead to surer judgement. And as the technique matures and experience and data are accumulated, so will rational decisions be assisted in the wise use of public investment resources.'[10]

The economic evaluation of transportation proposals

Road proposals[11]

The Ministry of Transport has produced several documents dealing with the techniques and problems associated with an economic assessment of road improvements. These have invariably been based on work done by the Road Research Laboratory, and current developments tend to be an elaboration of earlier work done by D. J. Reynolds.[12]

Three main stages are involved in an evaluation of the economic benefits associated with road improvements, (1) the estimation of the cost involved in an improvement scheme, (2) the estimation of the benefits, and their monetary value, derived from an improvement scheme, (3) the relation of the costs involved to the benefits derived.

1 *Costs:* The capital costs involved in any road improvement scheme should include the construction costs of the road, at the price level obtaining on the date on which the improvement is carried out; the cost of land acquisition, compensation, legal and administrative procedures, and maintenance costs. Land which has been acquired some time in advance of the date on which the improvement is to be carried out should be valued at its present alternative use value, whilst maintenance costs likely to prevail in the future should cover such aspects as the cost of periodic resurfacing, cleansing, lighting, verge maintenance and traffic control. If a complete discounted flow calculation rather than a first year rate of return is to be calculated then interest costs on work in progress should be omitted.

One further cost, which is often ignored in road improvement schemes, is the cost of delay and accidents imposed on road users whilst the improvement is being carried out. These costs are especially important if a discounted flow calculation is to be used as immediate costs are discounted less heavily than future long term benefits.

2 *Benefits and associated monetary values:* 'Road improvements are designed to bring benefits to road users in the form of cheaper, quicker and safer travel.'[13]

The relevant benefits include those resulting from the saving in time, and the reduction of accidents, and also a number of environmental or amenity benefits, such as the reduction in traffic noise or fumes. These amenity benefits are often difficult to quantify and impossible to put a monetary value to. Consequently they are generally excluded from an economic assessment of most road improvement schemes.

In considering the benefits derived from a road improvement four main categories of traffic must be distinguished—traffic already using the road to be improved; traffic likely to divert to the improved road from other roads; traffic which will remain on roads from which traffic will be diverted; and generated traffic. For all these categories it is essential to estimate the likely traffic flows, in terms of an annual average daily flow (be it 24, 16 or 12 hours), or an annual average hourly flow, to calculate the benefits due to changes in journey speed.

The average 24-hour flow can be derived in a variety of ways, e.g. by using continuous automatic counts for one year, or four continuous automatic counts for one week at three-monthly intervals, supplemented by manual counts.[14]

For evaluation purposes it is also necessary to have some measure of the likely future growth in traffic. The Road Research Laboratory has established that current growth rates in p.c.u.s are in the region of 5% per annum compound, and in the absence of known local factors recommend that this growth rate should be used. However, for long term improvements reference should be made to the latest available estimates on vehicle ownership and traffic growth.[15,16]

Savings in the operating costs can be subdivided into journey time savings and vehicle running costs. In assessing the journey time savings it is necessary to estimate accurately the difference in journey times between the existing unimproved and the proposed improved road. This involves measuring present-day speeds on the unimproved road, estimating how these speeds on the unimproved road would be likely to change with the growth of traffic; estimating the speeds likely to be achieved on the improved road and comparing the results to derive the journey time savings which would result from the improvement. Perhaps the most satisfactory method of measuring present day speeds or journey times on the unimproved road is the moving observer method previously described.[17] Up to 25 m.p.h. the speed of all traffic is considered to be the same. However, above 25 m.p.h. it is recognised that the average speed of private motor vehicles is likely to be higher than for other types of traffic. Consequently, adjustments are made to the average speed to take this into account. Between 25 m.p.h. and 39 m.p.h. it is assumed that the average speed for private motor vehicles is 1 m.p.h. more than the average speed for all traffic. Above 40 m.p.h., each 4 m.p.h. increase in the speed of all traffic is assumed to result in a 5 m.p.h. increase in private motor vehicle speeds.

Given an estimate of the traffic flows likely to use an improved road, the appropriate speeds on the new links can be calculated from the following empirically derived formulae.

(*a*) Central urban roads

$$V = 31 - \frac{q + 430}{3(w-6)} \quad \text{(or 24 m.p.h. whichever is the less)}$$

(*b*) Rural roads (single carriageway)

$$V = 51 - \frac{q + 1400}{6w} \quad \text{(or 43 m.p.h. whichever is the less)}$$

where V = running speed in m.p.h.
q = total flow in vehicles per hour.
w = carriageway width in feet.

For rural dual carriageway V is taken to be 48–50 m.p.h. and for motorways V is taken to be between 51–53 m.p.h.

The above formulae can be modified to take into account the effect of realignment, prolonged gradients, and to assess the increase of journey time likely to result from the growth of traffic and associated congestion, if the road were not improved.[18]

In urban areas improvements at intersections may be more important than improvements carried out on links between intersections. Changes in delay at intersections can again be calculated from standard formulae, based on empirical observations. In estimating the monetary value of the benefits derived from a change in operating costs both the vehicle operating and time-saving costs can be considered together, and the Road Research Laboratory has published standard formulae to calculate the average operating cost per vehicle mile.[19] They are

1
$$C = 4 \cdot 4 + \frac{218}{V}$$

where V is the average speed of all traffic and is less than 37 m.p.h. or

2
$$C = 5 \cdot 0 + \frac{196}{V}$$

where V is the average speed of all traffic and is in excess of 37 m.p.h.

C is the average operating cost per vehicle mile in pence.

These formulae are based on the assumption that non-working time is valued at three-quarters of working time and relate to the average composition of traffic on all roads in 1963 (69% cars and taxis, 3% buses and coaches, 14% light commercial vehicles and 14% other commercial vehicles). It does appear, however, that small divergences from the average composition do not materially affect the validity of these formulae. If no value is placed on non-working time the formulae are:

$$C = 4 \cdot 4 + \frac{93}{V} \text{ if } V \text{ is less than 37 m.p.h.}$$

or
$$C = 5 \cdot 0 + \frac{71}{V} \text{ if } V \text{ is greater than 37 m.p.h.}$$

Delays at intersections are valued at 218d. per vehicle hour (or 93d. per vehicle hour if no value is given to non-working time).

It should be noted, however, that the above estimates of operating costs are based on data relating to 1963 and which is out of date in some respects, e.g. the average hourly rate of pay may well have increased since 1963 resulting in an increase in the value to be placed on non-work time values.

Another basic criticism of the formulae is that it is difficult to put a value on non-work time anyway, although this can be overcome to some extent by using a range of values, as was done in the M1 study previously described.

The benefits resulting from a reduction in the number of accidents associated with road improvements can be estimated either from (1) an analysis of the results of before-and-after studies which have been carried out elsewhere to give an indication of the changes that can be expected from different types of improvement,[20] or (2) an examination of the accident rates on different classes of road.[21]

An average cost per personal injury accident is then applied to the estimated difference in the number of personal injury accidents. The current rate is £1,150 for each personal injury accident which reflects the cost of medical treatment, damage to property, loss of output and administrative expenses.

It could be argued that the above monetary value is an inadequate measure of accident cost as the severity, and hence cost, per personal injury accident would seem to increase with the speed at which traffic is able to travel. However, in the absence of a more sophisticated non-monetary statistic to represent accident savings, it must be used in a cautious way.

In addition to the traffic normally using the road, and the growth in traffic with time, a road improvement will often generate additional flows by making worth while under improved conditions, journeys which were not previously undertaken. In congested areas, where there is likely to be a frustrated demand ready to take advantage of any improvement on the highway system, this generated traffic can be of particular importance.

Estimates of this generated traffic are derived from a fundamental knowledge of the relationship between cost of travel and the volume of traffic. Attempts have been made to establish a general law expressing this relationship in the form of a gravity model. Thus:

$$Qij = \frac{k \; Pi \; Pj}{d^n}$$

Qij =traffic flow per unit of time by a given means of transport between i and j.
k =constant
$PiPj$=population of areas i and j
d =indication of cost of travel (usually distance or journey time)
n =a positive exponent.

The benefits to generated traffic are normally considered to be 50% of the benefits applied to traffic normally using the improvement.

3 Comparison of costs and benefits: There are two methods of presenting the final results comparing the costs and benefits associated with improvements. The simpler method involves the use of a 'first year rate of return' in which the costs of construction are discounted forward to the year of completion, and then compared with the benefits derived for the first year of operation of the completed scheme. The ratio of the annual benefit to the construction cost is expressed in percentage terms as the annual rate of return.

In equation form the rate of return may be expressed as

$$R = \frac{O + A - M}{C} \times 100$$

where R=Rate of return in %.
O=Savings in annual labour, vehicle time and operating costs.
A=Annual savings in costs of accidents.
M=Additional maintenence costs per annum.
C=Capital cost of improvement.

A more complicated approach can be adopted which takes account of the fact that future costs and benefits are worth less in the future than they are today. Using this technique, costs and benefits are calculated for each year for, say, thirty years and discounted back to the present day to give the net present value. The net present value is expressed as a percentage ratio of the discounted capital cost. If the net present value is positive it can be argued that the proposal is worth while.

Algebraically the present discounted value is expressed as

$$P_0 = (B_0 - C_0) + \frac{(B_1 - C_1)}{(1+i)} + \ldots\ldots + \frac{(B_n - C_n)}{(1+i)_n}$$

where P_0 = the present value of the investment in year o
B_0 and C_0 = benefits and costs in year o
$B_1 - B_n$ = benefits in years 1 to n
$C_1 - C_n$ = costs in years 1 to n
i = the discount rate per annum
n = the number of years for which the return is to be calculated

The present discounted value should always be accompanied by a 'first year rate of return' calculation, which should ideally be in excess of the rate of interest used in the present discounted value calculation. If the first year rate of return is less than the rate of interest used in the present discounted value calculation then the scheme should be postponed. This will have the effect of increasing the discounted value.

Railway operations

With exceptions the evaluation of rail schemes has to date taken the form of disinvestment rather than new investment proposals. Economic assessments have generally been undertaken with a view to closing down services rather than developing new routes. The techniques used in these evaluations are based on marginal cost accounting principles, and show the net financial benefit to British Rail resulting from line closures. With the exception of the social cost-benefit analyses undertaken in connection with the closure of certain lines in North Wales, social factors such as time loss and inconvenience to passengers are excluded from such economic assessments.

Rail investment proposals

Work done in connection with the Victoria Line underground railway, and the *Liverpool Outer Rail Loop Study*, have indicated in broad terms the approach which should be adopted in evaluating in economic terms rail investment proposals.

In such scheme the capital and operating costs should ideally be compared by some form of discounted cost flow calculation. However, such a calculation requires an estimate of both rail and road conditions well into the future, which may be impossible. As an alternative a simple annual first year rate of return can be used. The capital and operating costs of new rail proposals are generally easier to deal with than the associated benefits. Capital costs should be discounted back to a common base year, and operating costs will vary with the predicted level of traffic, and the increase in labour costs.

The benefits derived from such proposals are more difficult to cope with. Time savings, diverted and generated traffic benefits can be derived comparatively easily, but benefits associated with changes in comfort and level of service are much more difficult to assess and quantify. Other aspects which should be included in an evaluation of this kind include changes in income received by the public transport operators, and changes in Central Government revenue from indirect taxation such as fuel tax.

Evaluation of complete transportation network proposals

There are no absolute standards by which a transportation plan can be evaluated. It can only be compared with the estimated results likely to be achieved through the adoption of some other plan. This alternative plan can range from a 'minimum' plan in which nothing is done, at one extreme, to a comprehensive set of proposals at the other. General comparisons with the base year situation can be achieved by analysing simple tabulations such as trip totals by mode and purpose, and total inter-zonal movements.

A basic appreciation of how the proposed transport systems are likely to function can be derived from an examination of the 'loads' assigned to the different 'links' of the system, and comparing them with estimated capacities. In this particular respect an automatic data plotter operating in conjunction with computer output can quite rapidly plot a network of some size, showing link volumes or volume/capacity ratios.

To date the techniques adopted in an economic evaluation of transportation proposals for the large conurbations have regarded the total movement demands as a function of the proposed transport network. This contrasts with the simpler analyses already outlined where, with the exception of generated traffic, trips have been considered independent of the network and the benefits were derived direct from statistics relating to vehicle miles and time. The evaluation of user benefits derived from a complete transportation plan is more complex, and one possible approach could involve

1 an estimation of the volume of traffic moving between any two zones, for any given time period, both with and without the new transportation proposals

2 the calculation of the mean of the two volumes estimated above

3 the multiplication of this mean by the cost differential (i.e. the cost without minus cost with)

4 the summation of the total derived in (3) above, for all possible combinations of movement, to give the total direct user benefit during the chosen time interval.

This technique utilises the reduction in cost of travel likely to result from the transportation network proposals as a measure of the benefits users will receive, and cost in this context includes fares, vehicle operating costs, time, comfort and convenience.

In the analysis three types of journey should be considered:

1 journeys unaffected by the new proposals, i.e. journeys between the same origin and destination, by the same route and mode. These journeys will obtain some benefit (or incur further costs) depending on the ease (or increased difficulty) with which these trips can be made. This benefit or loss will be equivalent to the cost differential derived from the cost of trip making before and after the new proposals are introduced.

2 journeys generated by the new proposals, i.e. trips not

previously made, but which, because of the improved facilities, are now completed. As in the M1 and Victoria Line studies such trips are considered to benefit less than the already existing trips, and would be likely to be valued at 50% of the cost differential.

3 journeys which have changed their destination as a result of the improved facilities provided by the transport system, i.e. journeys which formerly went from A to B, now go from A to Z because under the base year situation it was difficult or impossible to get from A–Z, but the new proposals incorporate a link which allows journeys from A–Z to be incorporated.

This type of analysis is crude in the extreme, and presupposes that all travellers have the ability to estimate in advance the likely cost of any action they consider undertaking. However, from a practical point of view an averaging process is necessary, which reflects the different preferences, and values of different people.

One further complication arises from the fact that the same journeys can have different costs at different times of the day, by different modes of travel and for different journey purposes, e.g. a journey in the peak period may cost (in cost-benefit terms) considerably more than the same journey at midnight, whilst a journey undertaken for leisure purposes may 'cost' less than the same journey undertaken for business reasons. To overcome the problems associated with journeys undertaken for different purposes, by different modes and at different times of the day involves the same considerations, i.e. cost differential before and after the transport proposals should be introduced by the main journey purposes, e.g. leisure, to work, and commercial, and by the major modes of travel, e.g. public and private transport and for the most significant time periods, e.g. peak and off-peak periods.

The problems associated with the consideration of the same journey by different and competing modes is, however, slightly more complex, as each individual user will assess the cost of travel by competing modes in the light of his own preferences. It is assumed that he will only transfer to an alternative mode if the cost is less by that mode than the mode being used. Thus the benefit associated with a change of mode can be considered to be a function of both the cost of the previous mode, as well as the cost of the alternative mode. This could be taken into consideration, by relating the benefits derived from a change of mode to the ratio of the journey volumes using the competing modes before and after the introduction of the transportation proposals being evaluated.

The capital and operating costs involved in the implementation of the proposals, and the value of individual time savings can be deduced in the same way as they are estimated for normal road improvements.

The comparison of costs and benefits associated with complete urban transportation system proposals is usually expressed as a one-year rate of return since the expense and time involved in the production of a present discounted value is likely to be prohibitive.

References

1 Prest A. R. and Turvey R., *Cost-Benefit Analysis: A Survey*, Surveys of Economic Theory, Vol. III, Macmillan (1967).
2 Peters G. H., *Cost-Benefit Analysis and Public Expenditure*, Eaton Paper No. 8 (1968).
3 Peters G. H., *op. cit.*
4 Coburn T. M., Beesley M. E. and Reynolds D. J. The London–Birmingham Motorway—Traffic and Economics, *Road Research Technical Paper*, No. 46, H.M.S.O. (1960).
5 Coburn T. M., Beesley M. E. and Reynolds D. J., *op. cit.*
6 Reynolds D. J., The cost of road accidents, *Journal of the Royal Statistical Society*, Series A, General (1956).
7 Foster C. D. and Beesley M. E., Estimating the social benefit of constructing an underground railway in London, *Journal of the Royal Statistical Society*, Series A, General (1963).
8 Foster C. D. and Beesley M. E., The Victoria Line: social benefit and finances, *Journal of the Royal Statistical Society*, Series A, General (1965).
9 Buchanan C. D., *Traffic in Towns*, H.M.S.O., London (1963).
10 Buchanan C. D., *op. cit.*
11 Dawson R. F. F., The economic assessment of road improvement schemes; *Road Research Technical Paper*, No. 75. Ministry of Transport, H.M.S.O. (1968).

12 Reynolds D. J., The assessment of priorities for road improvements, *Road Research Technical Paper*, No. 48, H.M.S.O., London (1960).

13 *Research on Road Traffic*, Chapter 15, H.M.S.O., London (1965).

14 See: *Research on Road Traffic*, Chapter 2, H.M.S.O., London (1965).

15 See Ministry of Transport, Scottish Development Department. Urban Traffic Engineering Techniques, Para. 21, H.M.S.O., London (1965).

16 Road Research Laboratory, *Research on Road Traffic*, Chapter 2, *op. cit.*

17 Wardrop J. G. and Charlesworth G., A method of estimating speed and flow of traffic from a moving vehicle, *Proceedings Institution of Civil Engineers*, Part II (1954).

18 Road Research Laboratory, *Research on Road Traffic*, Chapter 15, *op. cit.*

19 Road Research Laboratory, *Research on Road Traffic*, Chapter 15, *op. cit.*

20 Road Research Laboratory, *Research on Road Traffic*, Chapter 11, *op. cit.*

21 Road Research Laboratory, *Research on Road Safety*, H.M.S.O., London (1965).

9   Conclusions

Historically the transportation planning process has developed using a series of models—namely trip generation, trip distribution, modal split, traffic assignment and network evaluation —and it is only by considering each of these models individually in some detail that a satisfactory understanding of the whole process can be best achieved. The obvious danger with such an approach is that it may tend to obscure the fact that each of the above models is an integral member of the whole—the transportation planning process is a system, made up of a range of different models which are in fact sub-systems within the main system. The very basis of the forecasting stage of the process is the interaction of each of the various individual models in the iterative process.

The transportation planning process is an expensive and time-consuming operation. It should also be a continuous process rather than a 'once and for all time' study, whereby regular comparisons should be made between actual and predicted land use and traffic developments. Any significant divergence between the actual and the forecasted developments should be analysed carefully to establish the reasons for the divergence and if necessary the original assumptions modified or amended to bring about a balance between the two values. Unfortunately, the early studies carried out in this country have proved to be expensive undertakings, which have invariably taken much longer to complete than the original estimated time. Consequently there is a danger that despite good intentions once these massive studies are finally completed, the bodies concerned may be too emasculated or bound up with the problems of implementing their plan proposals to carry out the necessary 'follow-up' studies.

Collection of basic data

The survey stage of the transportation planning process involves the accumulation of a considerable amount of basic movement and land-use data. This data is used to establish present-day relationships between movement and land use, to predict future land-use distribution and requirements and to develop the mathematical models used in the trip generation, trip distribution, modal split and assignment stages of the process.

Data collection and tabulation on this scale is expensive and time-consuming, requiring careful administration, and a considerable temporary labour force of no little intelligence. Yet the data collection procedures are well understood and documented, and are invariably the most thoroughly carried out stage of the whole transportation planning process. Indeed a basic criticism which can be levelled with some justification at many of the transportation studies carried out in this country is that too much basic data is collected, and that too many tabulations are produced from this data. This situation may well have arisen in Britain because of the need to gain experience in the administration and development of the new transportation planning techniques introduced from North America, with the result that people tended to be over-cautious and collect not only the basic data which was needed, but also other facts which looked as if they might be useful or interesting. Today those connected with the transportation planning process are well aware of this problem, and the extent of the unnecessary expense involved in the collection of too much data. Experience gained in the last few years has led to a much more critical assessment of what data should be collected, and the second generation studies now beginning are in general collecting or using only the information which will definitely be required in the later stages of the process. Perhaps the most significant step to be taken in reducing the survey stage to a more acceptable level is the use of the 1966 10% Sample Census data on workplace movements either in lieu of movement studies, or supplemented by limited movement surveys. As yet only one British transportation study—the *Tyneside Study* being undertaken by Alan Voorhees and Associates—is using this source of data, with considerable savings on cost. Research work into the potential use of this source of data in the transportation planning process is also being currently undertaken in the universities and in North America. One obvious way in which the survey stage of the process can be scaled down is to reduce the size of the home interview sample. Research work carried out at the University of North Carolina[1] investigating the effects of reducing sample sizes on the accuracy and reliability of trip generation by multiple linear regression analysis and trip distribution by gravity model has shown that although the error of prediction increases as the sample size decreases nevertheless it may be possible to produce reasonable results from more restricted surveys. However, further detailed research into this aspect is necessary before any definite conclusions can be drawn.

The number and range of the tabulations prepared from the basic survey data is invariably extensive and a good proportion of these are never used. This again probably stems from the same over-cautious approach adopted for the early studies when, rather than run the risk of omitting to investigate certain aspects of the movement pattern, any item which looked as if it might be significant was collected, collated, and tabulated, even if it was not subsequently analysed. Today this problem is not so pressing as experience has led to increased confidence on the part of the study organisers, who now collect and tabulate only the necessary data. Tabulations are kept to a basic minimum, although much effort is now expended in devising methods of storing the primary survey records in such a way that general purpose data retrieval computer programmes can be used to extract and prepare a whole range of tabulations should they be found necessary.

Prediction of Land-Use and Economic Data

'. . . the present round of (transport) studies . . ., whilst acknowledging the place of land use in travel generation, do little more than incorporate it as a control in the preparation of estimates of future travel needs.'[2]

The fundamental assumption on which the whole transportation planning process rests is that movement demands are directly related to the distribution and intensity of land uses, which are capable of being accurately predicted to some future date. The transportation side of the study is designed to answer two basic questions:

1 how much travel will there be in the future in the study area
2 where, within the study area, will this future travel be concentrated.

However, before these questions can be answered three basic land-use questions must also be answered:

1 How many people will be living in the study area in the future?
2 In what activities will they specifically be engaged, in an attempt to support themselves, and what will be their standard of living?
3 Where will the residential and non-residential space-using activities be located in the future?

To date, in Great Britain, it has been tacitly assumed that this is the province of the town planner and that he is eminently capable of providing satisfactory answers to the above questions. However, in practice it is generally found that this fundamental information, as the basis for a transportation study, is highly suspect. As his contribution to the team effort the planner invariably sees his task as one of collecting and collating on a traffic zonal basis a series of statistics based on often unrealistic Town Map or County Map proposals first put forward in the early and middle 1950s, often themselves based on false assumptions and prepared with only the crudest of prediction techniques. There are possibly two main reasons which could explain this situation. The first is that planning in Britain has, almost since its inception, been regulatory. The aim has been to plan to control what takes place in the future, rather than to plan to accommodate what takes place. Thus, it could be argued that if the regulatory powers are sufficiently strong it is of little importance, at least superficially, to be able to predict accurately what is likely to take place, as it is possible to control what actually takes place. Consequently the need to improve and develop more sophisticated prediction techniques for use in land-use planning has only recently been accepted by the more enlightened members of the profession.

The second reason which could possibly explain this situation is that many planners are not completely familiar with the transportation planning process. They are often misled and overawed by the apparent sophistication of the numerous mathematical techniques used in the different models, and are invariably unaware of the basic assumptions underlying these models. This lack of understanding and awareness of the significance of the land-use predictions in the transportation planning process, could well have led to the making of unrealistic future land-use predictions. Indeed, Proudlove has recently drawn attention to this problem when reviewing the *West Midlands Transportation Study*[3] by stating:

'This Study, and others in progress, reveal that transport study methodology is much more advanced and sophisticated than for land-use planning. The failure in the latter no doubt stems from the history of regulatory and non-constructive planning in Britain, and the failure to recognise the suscept- ibility of land use to market forces. The present inability of the land-use planner to match the technique of the transport planner renders invalid any study conclusions based on land- use predictions extending more than a few years beyond the present.'

The situation is a serious one. Official publications[4] empha- sise the need for considering land use and movement together in the preparation of town plans. Yet the ability to predict future movement desires and demands rests entirely on the ability to predict future land-use, population and economic characteristics. As yet the planning profession, with notable exceptions, has shown little awareness of the fact that town- plan proposals put forward on the basis of crude prediction techniques, and incorporating expensive highway and public transport proposals, could well prove in the long run to be inappropriate solutions to a set of problems which were completely misunderstood at the plan preparation stage. Before any significant progress can be made in the further development of land-use/transportation studies, improved land-use forecasting techniques must be developed, and a much greater understanding of the interrelationship of land development and the transport system reached. It is not as if there are no sophisticated prediction techniques available for the planner to adopt to meet his own needs. For many years now econometricians both in North America and Britain have been developing and improving techniques such as input-output analysis, linear programming, or analysis by the economic base multiplier method, which could be incorporated into the field of town and country planning quite readily, and would improve the forecasting process. Indeed these techniques have been used quite extensively in the development of regional and urban land-use models in the United States, and they are now beginning to be understood and used by planners in this country. The rate of progress is slow, however, and unless attempts are made to introduce and popularise these new techniques quickly much of the work at present being carried out on land-use/transport studies could well prove abortive in the long run.

Trip generation

Two basic forms of model have been developed to predict future levels of trip generation each utilising the observed relationships between movement and land use. They are multiple linear regression analysis and category analysis.

Multiple linear regression analysis is a well documented statistical and econometric prediction technique. It has been used in a whole range of different situations from business management to education. It is easy to understand and apply, especially with the use of standard computer programmes, and experience in transportation planning has shown that in the short term at least satisfactory predictions can be achieved. Although there are statistical problems associated with its use (e.g. a linear relationship must exist, each independent variable must have an additive effect), and although the basic assumptions which allow the technique to be used for forecasting are weak (coefficients established today hold good into the future; there is a causal relationship between the dependent and independent variables), nevertheless, multiple linear regression analysis is at present the most popular model for use in the prediction of future levels of trip generation.

Category analysis on the other hand avoids some of the criticisms levelled at multiple linear regression analysis. Its predictions are based on the assumption that trip generation rates exhibited today by different categories of household will hold good into the future. However, the problems posed for the planner in attempting to predict accurately on a zonal basis, up to 108 different categories of household, are enormous, and much work is required in the use and development of this technique before it can be accepted without reservation as a substitute for multiple linear regression analysis.

Trip distribution

Growth factor methods of distributing trips between the zones of the study area have been well used, tested and documented. Their reliability for short-term predictions in areas where little or no change is expected in the pattern and characteristics of land-use distribution is unquestioned. However, they cannot readily be applied in areas of change, where extensive development and redevelopment is likely to occur. It is in these areas that synthetic trip distribution models must be applied, and the choice of models available to the transportation planner is impressive, ranging from the gravity model, the linear regression model, and the opportunities models to the electrostatic field model.

The most popular and well-used model is the gravity model, possibly because it is comparatively easy to understand and apply, and in the short term, at least, has been found to give satisfactory results.

The opportunities models are more sophisticated and complex than the gravity model, and have been developed and used in some of the largest transportation studies carried out in North America and Britain. There are, however, problems associated with the use of this type of model, e.g. they can only account for a relative change in the time–distance relationship between all zones in a given urban area. Consequently their use, like the growth factor models, should be restricted to areas where no major changes are predicted. Comparison tests on the reliability of different trip distribution models has indicated that for all the increased complexity and sophistication of the opportunities models the results achieved are at best, no better than the simpler gravity and multiple linear regression models.

The multiple linear regression model can be used in the trip distribution stage of the transportation study. It is easy to understand and apply, and can incorporate any variable thought to have an influence on trip distribution. However, it has been little used for this purpose, largely because of the apparent need to prepare one equation for each pair of zones in the study area, a factor which is extremely expensive of computer time. Comparison tests of the different trip distribution models have shown that for the present-day situation the best results are achieved through the use of multiple linear regression techniques. This is not surprising when one considers that the predictive model is derived from the same data it is later asked to predict as a check.

Further research is needed into the use of multiple linear regression models in the trip distribution stage of the transportation planning process, especially into the possibility of reducing the number of different equations required.

The electrostatic field method of trip distribution is an interesting attempt to eliminate the need for expensive origin and destination studies in the transportation planning process, and as such warrants further research and development to allow its use in such a way that trips across an external cordon can be accommodated, and its accuracy of prediction improved. To date, because of these problems, the method has been little used.

Traffic assignment

The traffic assignment procedure is based on the selection of minimum time path over an actual route between each pair of zones in the study area. Three basic techniques are generally used—the diversion curve assignment, the all or nothing assignment, and the capacity restraint assignment—and although great advances have been made in the development of assignment procedures in the last decade many problems remain to be solved.

In theory the technique which approximates most closely to a real life situation is the capacity restraint assignment. In practice, in large urban areas, the results achieved through using this method have been far from satisfactory, and because of the iterative processes involved the faults and problems have been impossible to identify. The Department of Highways and Transportation of the Greater London Council have attempted to overcome the problems associated with the capacity restraint assignment by interrupting the computer programme and carrying out some of the assignment procedures manually. However, the basic problem associated with capacity restraint remains, i.e. the difficulty of finding any fundamental errors when checking assignments. Considerable research work is therefore necessary before it can be used with confidence.

The all or nothing assignment is a much cruder technique, which assigns traffic by the shortest route between two zones regardless of traffic volume and congestion on that route, although it has the advantage over capacity restraint in that it is comparatively simple to check and eliminate errors of over- or under-loading on any links. However, experience has shown all or nothing assignments when used on anything but the very smallest urban areas produce on occasions unusual results which can only be rectified by lengthy manual adjustments and reassignments.

Traffic assignment by the use of diversion curves is rarely attempted in large area transportation studies, where far reaching changes may be proposed for the transport system. However, in small urban areas where few changes are proposed they can be used quite successfully.

Despite the great advances made in the traffic assignment procedures recently, the application of the various techniques is not a straightforward matter. A considerable amount of professional skill is required on the part of the study staff to examine the frequently inaccurate all or nothing or capacity restraint assignments made by computer, to establish what the errors are, and to carry out the necessary adjustments and reassignments. In many instances it is often quicker and simpler to carry out a completely manual assignment. It is only when the area under study consists of a large number of zones that it is necessary and worth while to carry out an assignment by computer and then check and amend manually. Considerable further developments are necessary before traffic assignment procedures by computer are straightforward and reliable.

Modal split

Modal split—or the allocation of estimated future movements to alternative modes of transport—is perhaps the one aspect of the transportation planning process about which least is known. People are motivated to make their choice of travel mode for many reasons, only the most superficial of which can be identified and quantified. To date, many of the obvious factors influencing modal choice, such as time and cost of journey and journey purpose, have been assessed and quantified in some way. Other equally obvious influences on modal split such as comfort and convenience of competing modes of travel and the accessibility of one zone to another, have also been identified but have generally proved impossible to quantify adequately. There remains a possibly extensive range of other factors which subconsciously influence the individual's choice of travel mode. These factors could be highly individual and possibly irrational, yet they could collectively affect and influence the modal choice in a way which defies prediction. Although work is being carried out on modal split, considerably more attention must be given to this aspect, especially in the field of motivation studies, if it is to develop in conjunction with the other aspects of the total process.

Route location

Even if it is assumed that the transportation planning process, if properly conducted, will provide reliable estimates of the future scale and distribution of movement demand, the transportation engineer is still faced with the problem of where to route new major lines of communication through urban areas. The majority of the motorways already built in this country have been rural, and the traditional approach of considering only the road costs and road-user benefits in deciding upon a particular route has probably been adequate. However, as the transport problems of urban areas are gradually being tackled, so a much broader approach to the choice of route location is necessary—one which takes environmental factors into consideration, as well as construction costs and user benefits. A. Goldstein summarised the approach which should be adopted in the choice of route for a new line of communication which would be acceptable to the community at large when he stated:

'... where an optimum route is not self-evident, the surest way of obtaining this acceptance is to demonstrate that the best solution has been found by ... the full investigation of every reasonable alternative route ... and the preparation of a fully documented comparative evaluation giving facts and figures relating to each alternative and leading to the selection of a preferred route.'[5]

The problem is to devise a method of examining every possible alternative route without expending considerable staff and financial effort in the process. Work carried out recently by the staff of the Oxford City Corporation working in conjunction with transportation planning consultants has indicated the type of route location study which should be carried out as an integral part of the transportation planning process.[6] Briefly the method involves an examination for the whole of the study area, of those factors which could influence route location, e.g. engineering factors such as geology and land liable to flood; environmental factors such as the quality and use of open space; and the quality, use, age and condition of buildings. Each of these factors is given a weighting which reflects the importance of the particular factor. The study area is examined on a zonal basis and a 'score' given to each of the factors considered to influence route location, based on a subjective assessment by the surveyor. An aggregate score or route location weighting is derived for each zone, and this is taken as a reflection of the resistance to route location for that zone. By plotting the zone totals on a map of the study area 'contours of hardness' with respect to route location are derived.

From this map it is possible to eliminate the majority of alternative routes as being unsuitable for engineering and/or environmental reasons, leaving a reduced number of alternatives to be examined in greater detail.

The procedure is open to criticism on the grounds that it involves a purely subjective assessment of the factors influencing route location. However, it is a genuine attempt to consider all the factors which influence route location and as such deserves further consideration and research. It is likely that the use of this technique in similar circumstances by other bodies could result in the selection of different factors considered to influence route location, whilst different weightings could be allocated to the same factors in different circumstances. However, the more the technique is used the greater are the chances of deriving a set of factors and weightings which are a general consensus of opinion. Despite the subjective nature of the technique it has the advantage that it sets out in an ordered manner, in numerical short-hand form all the assessments made for each zone. It has the advantage of being easily modified, and it forces the team working on route location to think more deeply about the reasoning which has led to the subjective assessment of an area. The further development of this technique could well simplify the task of route selection, and of convincing the community at large that the route chosen is the best in the prevailing circumstances.

Economic evaluation

The techniques adopted to evaluate transport proposals vary with the scale of the works proposed. Limited improvements and developments which have only minor side effects can usually be quite readily measured, the costs and benefits associated with the proposal assessed, and a rate of return estimated.

The larger scale transportation proposals, such as the Victoria Line tube proposals in London, have generally far-reaching side effects, especially in the social field with the result that the costs and benefits associated with a particular project are much more difficult to assess, and a rate of return on the money invested almost impossible to estimate.

As an aid to orderly decision making the technique of cost-benefit analysis has been adapted from the field of economics and developed in the context of transportation planning. At the moment this technique is used very crudely, but despite criticisms from the economists, attempts have been made to quantify and value social costs and benefits associated with transportation proposals. The lead set by the 'Traffic in Towns' team[7] in attempting to evaluate all the costs and benefits associated with a proposal has not yet been followed up by further research, or application, yet such work is vital if the decision as to whether one project should be adopted at the expense of another is to be taken completely out of the realm of individual whim and personal preference.

Despite the fact that the transportation planning process can be broken down into a series of separate models these are in fact part of one major system and should be considered as such.

Significant advances in the development of the transport stages of the process have been achieved in recent years, yet the weakest part of the whole procedure is the land use, and economic forecasting stage which is really fundamental to the whole process. Although many of the different models which go to make up the over-all model appear to be complex and sophisticated, the assumptions on which they are based are at present weak. The transportation planning process is not the precise tool that some people like to think it is. Rather it is a rational process, which isolates all those factors which apparently influence movement demands, and attempts to present a logically argued case for estimating future movement demands. Despite the imperfections and weaknesses inherent in the process, it is an essential and integral part of town and country planning which continues to develop with time.

References

1 Horn J. W., *Examination and Comparison of A.D.T. Gravity Models*, Project ERD–110–X, Part II, University of North Carolina (1966).
2 Proudlove J. A., Some comments on the West Midlands Transport Study, *Traffic Engineering and Control* (1968).
3 Proudlove J. A., *op. cit.*
4 See Ministry of Transport Roads Circular No. 1/68. *Traffic and Transport Plans*, H.M.S.O., London (1968).
5 Goldstein A., Motorway Route Location, *Proceedings of the Town and Country Planning School* (1966).
6 Whittle R. J., *Route Location in Oxford*, unpublished paper presented at Symposium of the Institution of Municipal Engineers, Andover (1968).

Glossary

Assignment—When estimating traffic flows between an origin and a destination, and there is a choice of route available, then an *assignment* to the alternative routes must be made.

Cost-benefit study—A study designed to assist in choosing between alternative schemes where different levels of expenditure and different degrees of benefit are involved.

Desire Line, desire line diagram—A desire line is a straight line drawn on a map between two points to indicate a desire for a journey to be made between those points. It does not indicate the actual route of the journey.

A desire line diagram is used in practice to summarise the desires for movement between specified zones, lines between identical pairs of zones being grouped together so that the composite width of the group of lines is in proportion to the total number of desired movements.

Diverted Traffic—Traffic which has changed from its previous route of travel to another route, without change in origin or destination.

Environmental Area—An area having no extraneous traffic and within which considerations of environment predominate over the use of vehicles.

Freeway—The American equivalent of a motorway. Other terms are also used to describe high capacity roads such as *expressway,* or *through-way,* some of which indicate varying standards of design.

Generated Traffic (as used in Cost-benefit studies)—Traffic which did not previously exist in any form but which results when additional facilities are provided or existing facilities are improved. An alternative term used to describe the same feature is *Induced Traffic.*

Origin and Destination Survey—A survey to determine the origins and destinations of journeys.

Peak Hour—In respect of any road the period of one hour's duration in the 24-hour day during which the greatest amount of traffic is carried. In practice it is usual to distinguish morning, midday or evening peak-hours.

Screen Line—An imaginary line drawn across part of a traffic study area, across which the total number of movements of any particular kind are determined, in order to check the estimated traffic flows across the same line.

Traffic management—The promotion of a more efficient movement of traffic within a given street system by re-arranging the flows, controlling the intersections and regulating the times and places of parking.

Transportation Study—A comprehensive study of all the demands for movement in a locality to provide a basis for a co-ordinated planning of transport systems. Such a study involves the use of origin and destination surveys, home-interview surveys and other investigations.

Trip—A one-way movement between a point of origin and a point of destination.

Index